T0013081

PRAYER
POWER

PRAYER POWER

40 DAYS OF LEARNING TO PRAY LIKE GEORGE MÜLLER

BRENT PATRICK McDOUGAL

WHITAKER
HOUSE

Unless otherwise indicated, all Scripture quotations are taken from the *Holy Bible, New International Version*®, NIV®, © 1973, 1978, 1984, 2011 by Biblica, Inc.® Used by permission of Zondervan. All rights reserved worldwide. www.zondervan.com. The "NIV" and "New International Version" are trademarks registered in the United States Patent and Trademark Office by Biblica, Inc.® Scripture quotations marked (ESV) are taken from *The Holy Bible, English Standard Version*, © 2016, 2001, 2000, 1995 by Crossway Bibles, a division of Good News Publishers. Used by permission. All rights reserved. Scripture quotations marked (NLT) are taken from the *Holy Bible, New Living Translation*, © 1996, 2004, 2015 by Tyndale House Foundation. Used by permission of Tyndale House Publishers, Inc., Carol Stream, Illinois 60188. All rights reserved. Scripture quotations marked (KJV) are taken from the King James Version of the Holy Bible. Scripture quotations marked (NKJV) are taken from the *New King James Version*, © 1982 by Thomas Nelson, Inc. Used by permission. All rights reserved.

Boldface type in the Scripture quotations indicates the author's emphasis.

PRAYER POWER
40 Days of Learning to Pray Like George Müller

bmcdougal@fbcknox.org

ISBN: 978-1-64123-894-6
eBook ISBN: 978-1-64123-895-3

Printed in the United States of America
© 2022 by Brent Patrick McDougal

Whitaker House
1030 Hunt Valley Circle
New Kensington, PA 15068
www.whitakerhouse.com

Library of Congress Control Number: 2022942538

No part of this book may be reproduced or transmitted in any form or by any means, electronic or mechanical—including photocopying, recording, or by any information storage and retrieval system—without permission in writing from the publisher. Please direct your inquiries to permissionseditor@whitakerhouse.com.

1 2 3 4 5 6 7 8 9 10 11 **W** 29 28 27 26 25 24 23 22

CONTENTS

SECTION SIX: PERSIST IN PRAYER

INTRODUCTION

Prayer is the key that unlocks every door.

Your greatest resource is not money, intellect, popularity, or pedigree. Your greatest asset is not represented on your resume or in the roll call of your accomplishments. While all of these are good, they're secondary to the central, sacred resource available to you.

Prayer is the master key that rests among all of the other keys. Prayer does what none of these other keys can do. It opens the heart, opens possibilities that are impossible by natural means, and opens the door to God's presence.

Through prayer, peace and power flow from God into our lives. But it's not just any kind of prayer that you and I need. We need to learn a particular and persistent kind of prayer. We need to learn the conditions of prayer that prevail so that we can walk in faith, expecting answers and giving thanks even before prayer is answered.

You're invited into a forty-day journey to discover that kind of prayer.

Each day will feature a teaching from Scripture about prayer and a story or teaching from the life of one of my heroes of the faith, the nineteenth-century pastor George Müller.

Müller was born on September 27, 1805, in a city called Kroppenstaedt, which was then in the Kingdom of Prussia. For most of his ministry,

Müller pastored in Bristol, England. However, his work didn't stay within the walls of the church building. He launched orphanages that would provide shelter, food, education, and spiritual guidance for over ten thousand orphans. He also supported missionaries financially and distributed the Bible around the world.

> **THE WONDERFUL PROMISES IN THE BIBLE REGARDING PRAYER ARE AVAILABLE FOR EVERY BELIEVER TODAY AND IN EVERY AGE.**

A central element ran through Müller's life and ministry. He believed that the wonderful promises in the Bible regarding prayer were not just for the past or for a coming age. Instead, he believed they are available for every believer in the present. Müller studied the seemingly unbelievable teachings of Jesus on prayer and decided to apply them to all circumstances. He took Jesus at His word when He taught:

> *Ask and it will be given to you; seek and you will find; knock and the door will be opened to you. For everyone who asks receives; the one who seeks finds; and to the one who knocks, the door will be opened.*
>
> (Matthew 7:7–8)

The promise was not just for some but for everyone. If Jesus is to be believed, the door will swing wide for everyone who knocks.

"Why should not the believer always draw near to God in full confidence that he will do as he said?" asks Müller. "Our difficulty seems to be this: the promise is so 'exceedingly great'[1] that we cannot conceive God really to mean what he clearly appears to have revealed. The blessing seems too vast for our comprehension; we 'stagger at the promises, through unbelief,'[2] and thus fail to secure the treasure which was purchased for us by Christ Jesus."[3]

---

1. See 2 Peter 1:4 KJV.
2. See Romans 4:20 KJV.
3. George Müller, *The Life of Trust: Being a Narrative of the Lord's Dealings With George Müller*, accessed at www.gutenberg.org/files/27288/27288-h/27288-h.htm.

Since first learning about George Müller around twenty years ago, I have often shared stories about his life with others. I have used examples from his life to point people to a deeper experience of prayer.

Something happened to me, however, as I was sharing a story about answered prayer with bread and milk in one of Müller's orphanages. I thought, *I'm tired of telling stories about others and answered prayer. I want that kind of experience for myself. I want to know God's power and see if the promises are for me too.*

I started to dig more deeply into Müller's life, primarily through his autobiographical narrative called *The Life of Trust*. This narrative was written not only to help followers of Jesus believe that God's promises are for them but also to instruct them on the conditions leading to answered prayer. These conditions include abiding daily in God, relying on God in humble dependence, forsaking sin, exercising faith, seeking to do God's will, and persisting in prayer.

I began to put it into practice. I started each day with a prayer of simple reliance. I asked God to give me faith that His promises were indeed true. I journaled prayer requests and expected help. I examined areas of my life where I lacked faith or held onto small or large sins that created a huge chasm between me and God.

The impact was immediate. I began seeing more answers to prayer as my faith grew. With each promise fulfilled, I took a step of faith, leading me to pray even more.

Now I want to share with you what I have learned and continue to learn. You, too, can experience God's promises and the life-changing release of the power of prayer described in Müller's narrative.

A SIMPLE PRAYER LIFTS THE FOG

In 1877, Müller crossed the Atlantic from Newfoundland to Quebec for a preaching event. During the voyage, an unexpected, heavy fog descended and delayed the ship considerably. The ship's captain was a nominal Christian who had little experience with prayer. He had been on the bridge for twenty-two hours straight, worried and afraid for the crew and passengers.

All of a sudden, the captain felt a tap on his shoulder. It was Müller.

"Captain, I have come to tell you that I must be in Quebec on Saturday afternoon," said Müller.

"It is impossible," said the captain.

"Very well," replied Müller. "If your ship can't take me God will find some other means…I have never broken an engagement in fifty-seven years."

The captain said, "I would willingly help you, but how can I? I am helpless."

Müller invited the captain to go down to the chart room and pray. The captain thought he was crazy but followed him to the chart room.

"Mr. Müller, do you know how dense this fog is?" pressed the captain.

"No," Müller said, "my eye is not on the density of the fog, but on the living God, who controls every circumstance of my life." He then went down on his knees and prayed one of the simplest prayers the captain had ever heard: "O Lord, if it is consistent with Thy will, please remove this fog in five minutes. You know the engagement You made for me in Quebec for Saturday. I believe it is Your will." The captain thought this sounded like the prayer of a child.

When Müller concluded his prayer, the captain said he would pray as well, but Müller told him not to do so.

"First," he said, "you do not believe God will do it; and, second, I believe He has done it. And there is no need whatever for you to pray about it."

The captain stared in amazement. Müller continued, "Captain, I have known my Lord for fifty-seven years and there has never been a single day that I have failed to gain an audience with the King. Get up, Captain, and open the door, and you will find the fog is gone."

The captain got up. He opened the door. The fog was gone.

On Saturday afternoon, George Müller was in Quebec.[4]

Do you want that kind of faith? Are you ready to use the key that is already in your hand?

4. The George Müller website, "My Eye Is Not on the Fog," accessed August 13, 2021, www.georgemuller.org/devotional/my-eye-is-not-on-the-fog2874126.

THREE INGREDIENTS FOR POWERFUL PRAYER

Before you begin the forty-day journey of prevailing, powerful prayer, you'll need three things: a passion, a place, and a plan.

1. PASSIONATE BELIEF

First, you'll need to have a passion for prayer and for a deeper experience with God. You need to be tired of life as usual. You need a desire to make a change, wherever the journey leads. This journey can change your life just as it changed mine. But a halfhearted approach will yield no results.

We can receive wisdom—that is, a higher revelation and a deeper understanding—when we ask God for it and believe that He will grant our request.

James, the brother of Jesus, wrote:

You should ask God, who gives generously to all without finding fault, and it will be given to you. But when you ask, you must believe and not doubt, because the one who doubts is like a wave of the sea, blown and tossed by the wind. That person should not expect to receive anything from the Lord. (James 1:5–7)

This journey must start with a passionate belief. It must begin with faith and not doubt about the power of prayer and a simple faith in the One who hears prayer.

2. A QUIET PLACE TO PRAY

Second, you'll need a quiet, sacred place to pray. Jesus taught that such a place is essential. In the Sermon on the Mount, He said:

But when you pray, go into your room, close the door and pray to your Father, who is unseen. Then your Father, who sees what is done in secret, will reward you. (Matthew 6:6)

Jesus contrasted this prayer practice with what He saw in other religious leaders. They stood on street corners to pray or launched into lengthy, pious prayers to impress others. They liked to be seen. Jesus said they have their reward: the applause of other human beings. (See Matthew 6:5.)

It's likely that the type of prayer evident in Müller's life and described in this book has never been modeled for you. You may have only seen and heard prayers that seem somewhat hesitant, lacking faith, or ritualistic. You may have felt that there is a level of prayer that is just beyond your grasp.

The disciples said to Jesus, *"Lord, teach us to pray"* (Luke 11:1). They recognized that they needed to be taught how to pray. Jesus gave them a model prayer we know as "the Lord's prayer" or "the Our Father," but He also counseled them to go into a private room and close the door. God, who is unseen, would see what they had done in secret and reward them.

In a secret place, we meet more than a distant, uncaring deity. There we encounter our Father. When Jesus used the personal word "Father," He invited His followers to believe in a close, caring, generous God who loves them like children.

Each day, we need time in a quiet place where we can talk in intimate words with the living God who loves us. In that secret place, we can ask for what we need and then open the door to a day of possibilities. We can center our hearts again and again throughout the day, asking for what we need and trusting that God is willing to supply it all.

Could it really be true *for you* when Jesus says, *"Ask and it will be given to you"* (Matthew 7:7)? Can you really believe Jesus when He says, *"If you have faith and do not doubt…you can say to this mountain, 'Go, throw yourself into the sea,' and it will be done. **If you believe, you will receive whatever you ask for in prayer"*** (Matthew 21:21–22)? Were these promises only for the first disciples? In the secret place, you'll discover that the promises are for you too.

3. A BIBLE READING PLAN

Finally, you'll need a plan. While these devotions are intended to encourage faith, they are not a substitute for Scripture reading. You can use these devotions each day as a complement to a regular Bible reading plan. If you don't have such a plan, you could begin by reading a psalm each day and then a chapter from one of the Gospels. There are also many good Bible reading plans, such as the Moravian Daily Texts, that can help you implement a regular time of study.

The following is a simple plan:

+ Begin with a prayer that asks God to open your mind and heart to the teaching of Scripture, being led by the Holy Spirit.

+ Read your Scripture passages for the day.

+ Read a chapter of this devotional.

+ Pray until you come to a place of experiencing God's presence and peace.

+ Ask for what you need, turning your day over to God.

Do you trust that God delights in granting your requests for anything that is for your benefit, especially when you ask according to His will and for His glory?

Do you believe the key that unlocks all the doors is already in your hand?

For the next forty days, make it a priority to go into your secret room. Seek the living God. Immerse yourself in God's Word. Ask for what you need.

Then get up, open the door, and see what God will do.

SECTION ONE

ABIDE IN GOD

1

OPEN WIDE

Open wide your mouth and I will fill it.
—Psalm 81:10

When I began pastoring a church in Dallas, Texas, I believed two things: the sky was the limit; and the task was tremendous. We needed to rebuild a core of spiritual leaders, renovate most of our space, and renew our commitment to living in the power of the Holy Spirit. It was a God-sized opportunity.

Our maintenance supervisor, Juan, took me on a tour of the building, including the basement under the sanctuary, where I heard the faint sound of running water and wondered where it was coming from.

"There's a stream that runs under the church," Juan said. "When it rains, we can hear the water flowing under the sanctuary."

Symbolically, that's gold for a church that needs revitalization. A few leaders had already recognized the need to re-dig old wells of prayer and faith. (See Genesis 26:18.) We began to pray that God's Spirit would fill our sanctuary from the top of the rafters to the deep stream below.

We saw so many spiritual blessings in those first years in Dallas. We prayed that God would break down walls of racism, classism, and sexism. God brought the walls down. Baptisms happened almost every week. People who were addicted to drugs and alcohol turned to Christ. Teachers and other leaders were raised up. Some were sent out as missionaries. During those joy-filled days, I often thought of Psalm 126:1 (NLT): *"When the* LORD *brought back his exiles to Jerusalem, it was like a dream!"*

But God had even more in store. One of our biggest challenges was in the area of finances. We prayed that God would bring more resources and that we would be ready to steward those resources well. We had no idea, however, the blessings that we would receive.

A WELLSPRING OF GENEROSITY FLOWS

I had been there for about eighteen months when God cracked open the heart of our church in a wellspring of generosity. For ten years, the church had an annual deficit in giving. It was a real faith-killer. Each year, the church came up short after pleading for more to be given, with regular givers complaining about having to shoulder too much of the load. However, as that year ended and we challenged people to give, we finished with a $250,000 surplus. We dedicated 75 percent of that money to missions and set aside the rest for building renovations.

We were elated. But the truth was that we needed fifty times that amount to renovate our spaces. So we kept praying.

One day, our church administrator, Brad, called me and said someone had left some money to the church in a will. It was big, he said. Maybe over a million dollars. By the time all of the assets were distributed, the gift was three and a half million dollars. It allowed us to make some much-needed repairs and renovate our main fellowship space.

We then challenged the church to match the gift and go beyond the remaining amount, raising another two and a half million. As the spaces were renovated, our faith grew.

God deserves all the credit, glory, and praise for what happened during my decade in Dallas. I couldn't take credit if I tried. I do believe, however, that both seeking the Lord and asking for help in faith were crucial.

How much faith do you have? Is there enough to dream big?

Do you even ask for what you need, believing that God will provide?

When the idea of establishing an orphanage entered George Müller's mind, for the first two weeks, he prayed that God would bring it about only if it was God's will. If it was not God's dream, then Müller asked that God would graciously remove the thought from his mind. He knew that God would be pleased in caring for fatherless and motherless children, but he didn't know if God wanted *him* to be the instrument to bring it about.

GEORGE MÜLLER DIDN'T ASK FOR PROVISIONS, PLANS, OR PEOPLE FOR AN ORPHANAGE. HE ONLY ASKED THAT GOD WOULD CONFIRM WHETHER IT WAS HIS WILL.

Therefore, he didn't ask for provisions, plans, or people to work in the orphanage. He only asked that God would confirm whether it was His will.

But on December 5, 1835, Müller's prayers had changed:

I was reading Psalm 81 and was particularly struck, more than at any time before, with verse 10: 'Open thy mouth wide, and I will fill it.' I thought a few moments about these words and then was led to apply them to the case of the orphan-house. It struck me that I had never asked the Lord for anything concerning it, except to know His will...I then fell on my knees and opened my mouth wide, asking Him for much. I asked in submission to His will and without fixing a time when He should answer my petition. I prayed that He would give me a house, either as a loan or that someone might be led to pay the rent for one or that one might be given permanently for this object; further, I asked Him for [one thousand pounds] and likewise for suitable individuals to take care of the children.[5]

5. George Müller, "Prayer and My Orphans," *The King's Business*, April 1957, 16–17.

First, notice that Müller didn't pray for funds first. He didn't start with a laundry list of what he thought was required. Instead, he asked God to reveal whether He wanted to use Müller for this purpose.

Second, notice that when Müller began to pray, he knew how to pray. He literally opened his mouth and out came the words that glorified God as His servant asked for what he needed.

Eighteen months later, Müller noted in his journal that the last five pounds had been given to complete God's gift of a thousand pounds to the orphanage. On June 15, 1837, Müller reflected:

> From the moment I asked till the Lord granted it fully, I had never been allowed to doubt that he would give every shilling of that sum. Often have I praised him beforehand, in the assurance that He would grant my request.[6]

Müller knew that he had no natural prospects of receiving the income. He didn't know how the money would come, but he trusted that God would provide it. He believed that when he opened his mouth wide, God would fill it.

THREE PRAYER MISSTEPS

I wonder if sometimes we make one of three missteps when it comes to prayer.

The first is to rush in too quickly to ask for what we think we need. We don't pause and pray long enough to consider whether what we want is what God wants. As a result, we're left disappointed in prayer and wondering if our dream is not the will of God.

The second misstep is to fail to open our mouths wide—really wide—so that God can fill us and bless others through us in a tremendous way. Once we know what God wants, we should not be afraid to ask for what we need to fulfill that plan.

The third misstep is to fail to give God praise when the blessings come. How many blessings have you taken for granted? How often has God given you a good gift, only to see you take the credit for yourself?

6. Müller, *The Life of Trust.*

It's been said that any blessing we don't turn back to praise turns into pride. Many times when God blessed us in Dallas, I was tempted to believe that we deserved or earned it.

> **ONCE WE KNOW WHAT GOD WANTS, WE SHOULD NOT BE AFRAID TO ASK FOR WHAT WE NEED TO FULFILL THAT PLAN.**

The key to faithful prayer is found in knowing that you and I have no natural prospect of gaining what God wants to provide. It's all grace. It all belongs to Him. Everything you are and everything you have is given by the grace of God.

I don't know how God wants to bless you, but I do know that like the sanctuary in Dallas, underneath your life is a deep stream of God's blessing. God wants to fill you from that stream.

In Genesis 26:2–5, God appeared to Isaac and told him to remain in the Philistine land of Gerar, where God would bless Isaac because his father, Abraham, had been faithful to keep God's laws. Isaac indeed was prosperous, but there was a problem. All of Abraham's wells had been filled in by the Philistines.

Water was essential to sustain Isaac's family and flocks. To dwell in the land, *"Isaac reopened the wells that had been dug in the time of his father Abraham, which the Philistines had stopped up after Abraham died, and he gave them the same names his father had given them"* (Genesis 26:18).

Prayer is the well that taps into God's stream of blessings.

Maybe your prayer today is, "God, You created me to dream big. Help me to pray God-sized dreams. I want to know how to pray according to Your will, for Your glory."

If not that, then perhaps your prayer is, "God, today I am opening my mouth wide that You would fill it. My mouth is opened so that praises and thanksgiving can flow out. Fill me with everything You desire so that I can bless others."

Or maybe your prayer today is, "God, You made me for Your glory. You have given me the gift of prayer to connect with You and to offer You praise. Help me to open again the ancient well deep within my soul so that Your living water can satisfy me and I can return praises to Your name."

Now is the time to pray.

Dream big.

Wait for God to reveal if your dream is God's dream.

Ask for what you need.

God is waiting for you.

PRAYER PRINCIPLE #1:

God can't fill a closed mouth.

2

HAPPY IN THE LORD

*If you abide in me, and my words abide in you, ask whatever you
wish, and it will be done for you.*
—John 15:7 ESV

ESPN posted an intriguing story entitled "Whatever Happened to
Villanova Basketball Star Shelly Pennefather?"[7] Shelly was a standout.
Since the late 1980s, she has held Villanova's all-time scoring record for
women and men, without the benefit of the three-point shot. Shelly had a
contract offer to play in Japan as one of the highest paid women's basketball
stars at the time.

Shelly was more than an athlete. When she walked into a room, it
came alive because of her cheerfulness and confidence. Everyone knew that
she was going to be a remarkable leader.

That's why the sports world was shocked when on July 8, 1991, Shelly
and her family left her home and drove to the monastery of the Poor Clares
in Alexandria, Virginia. She was greeted by fifteen nuns who accepted her

---

7. Elizabeth Merrill, "Whatever happened to Villanova basketball star Shelly Pennefather?"
ESPN, accessed August 15, 2021, www.espn.com/womens-college-basketball/story/_/
id/27297631/happened-villanova-basketball-star-shelly-pennefather-made-deal-god.

into their convent. As the door closed, Shelly knew that she was cut off from both the world and her family.

One of the strictest religious orders in the world, the Poor Clares sleep in full habit on straw mattresses. They wake up every night at 12:30 a.m. to pray and never rest for more than four hours at a time. Cut off from society, the Poor Clares remain silent and barefoot twenty-three hours a day, wearing sandals for just one hour of walking. Shelly will never leave the monastery. She'll never call or email or text anyone. She gets two family visits a year but can only converse through a screen. And once every twenty-five years, she can hug her family.

Genuinely perplexed, the author of the ESPN article wondered, "Why would someone with so much to offer the world lock herself away and hide her talents?" Shelly had left Villanova to go to Japan with a salary of $200,000, but she was intensely lonely and restless in Japan. She believed that God was calling her to something greater.

HEARING THE CALL TO ABIDE

Shelly was attending a retreat when she was asked to read aloud the words of Jesus from John 6:56: "*Whoever eats my flesh and drinks my blood remains in me, and I in him.*" *Remain* is the same as *abide*. When Shelly read those words, it hit her: she felt that God was right there, twenty feet in front of her. She kept reading. When she closed her Bible, she said a silent prayer and then sat in stunned silence. From that day on, she knew she was no longer alone. She felt that the seed of a radical call from God had been planted in her. To enter the convent was the highest ideal she could aspire to—total devotion to God—and she did it.

An ESPN reporter was present when twenty-five years after taking her vows, the convent chapel's two wooden doors opened. Everyone in the chapel gasped as Shelly, then fifty-three years old, walked in and stood before them with no screen. She renewed her vows, hugged her family in tears, and then returned to her cloistered life for another twenty-five years.

During her encounter with her family and former teammates, she told them, "I love this life. I wish you all could just live it for a little while just to see. It's so peaceful. I just feel like I'm not underliving life. I'm living it to the full."

So many people are "underliving" life, mostly because they are not brave enough to follow the summons of God to a great adventure.

> **SO MANY PEOPLE ARE "UNDERLIVING" LIFE, MOSTLY BECAUSE THEY ARE NOT BRAVE ENOUGH TO FOLLOW THE SUMMONS OF GOD TO A GREAT ADVENTURE.**

This call doesn't make sense to most people. Those who accept the call often disappoint loved ones who are close to them. Those who follow the Spirit of Christ don't act like others. They trust an inner voice, a gentle wind to guide them.

Accepting this call is painful at first but then feels like sliding along with the grain of the wood. It's like coming home. It's like breathing. There's a deep assurance that settles in when someone abides in the Spirit.

In his little devotion called *The Spirit of Christ*, Andrew Murray says:

> The leading of the Spirit does not begin in the region of thought or feeling. The Holy Spirit makes His home deeper down in the life itself. In this hidden laboratory of the inner life is the power that molds the will and fashions the character in our spirit. There He breathes and moves and guides.[8]

George Müller lived in quiet dependence upon his heavenly Father. He believed that if he walked with God and expected help from God, God would never fail him. He also committed himself to depend completely on God for all that he needed. Day by day, he trusted the Lord. Day by day, God provided. Sometimes he woke up with no means to buy bread for his family or the children of his orphanage. But as needs arose, God arrived at the right time.

---

8. Andrew Murray, *The Spirit of Christ* (New Kensington, PA: Whitaker House, 1984), 147.

People often remarked to Müller, "How can you live this way? This must be a very trying life. You must be tired of it." This was Müller's reply as stated in his autobiographical narrative:

> I do not find the life in connection with this work a trying life, but a very happy one. It is impossible to describe the abundance of peace and heavenly joy that often has flowed into my soul by means of the fresh answers which I have obtained from God, after waiting upon him for help and blessing; and the longer I have had to wait upon him, or the greater my need was, the greater the enjoyment when at last the answer came, which has often been in a very remarkable way, in order to make the hand of God the more manifest.[9]

Is this kind of life just for the super-saints, or is it available to all of us?

Jesus said the key to such happiness is abiding in Him. Not only is such a life available to all of us, but *we were created for such a happy life*. God's desire is to make a home inside of us such that whenever a need arises, we can ask God and trust that need will be met. If it is not, then we can trust that God will meet it or give us something better in His time.

Think of God like a big house. Jesus said, *"My Father's house has many rooms"* (John 14:2). The life of faith is an invitation to explore that house.

Ironically, many people are afraid that if they lean into faith—if they devote more time to prayer and make abiding their central task—then they will be "underliving." They believe they will feel limited and less than fulfilled.

That's what the world assumes, but the opposite is true. Jesus said, *"Let anyone who is thirsty come to me and drink"* (John 7:37). He said, *"My flesh is real food and my blood is real drink"* (John 6:55).

The most important thing to know about yourself is that you were made to live in God. You have a soul. A soul that doesn't drink of the greatness and power and justice and holiness and love of God will die of thirst. A soul that doesn't feast daily on the living God will waste away, undernourished and unsatisfied.

---

9. Müller, *The Life of Trust*.

Abiding involves a kind of ordering of your day whereby you make sure you are drinking in His Spirit and enjoying His true food. It means living a life that experiences the promise of Psalm 34:8 (ESV): *"Oh, taste and see that the LORD is good!"*

FIVE IDEAS TO ORDER YOUR LIFE

Most of us will never live a cloistered life. But perhaps we need a kind of *rule* that allows us to operate differently from the rest of the world. Here are five ideas to order your life:

1. Go early each day into your private place. God waits for you to bring every need to Him. Believe that God will reward you in secret. Believe Jesus when He says, *"I will do whatever you ask in my name, so that the Father may be glorified in the Son"* (John 14:13).

2. *"Whatever you do, work at it with all your heart, as working for the Lord"* (Colossians 3:23).

3. Expect that on occasion, God will call you to something new, maybe even something radical, maybe at an age that you didn't expect.

4. Don't expect that the window of opportunity will always be open. When the Holy Spirit whispers to you and you push Him away again and again, God will eventually use someone else. You might find yourself wondering if you know what the voice of God sounds like at all. When the window or the door opens, take it.

WHEN THE HOLY SPIRIT WHISPERS TO YOU AND YOU PUSH HIM AWAY AGAIN AND AGAIN, GOD WILL EVENTUALLY USE SOMEONE ELSE.

5. Do some righteous act every week to care for the poor or the marginalized. If you don't, you probably aren't living by the Spirit of Christ because Jesus was always caring for such people. You'll

meet Him in the faces of broken people, strangers, and those who are weak.

Jesus said, "*I have come that they may have life, and have it to the full*" (John 10:10).

Can you say, like Shelly Pennefather, that you are living life to the full?

You, too, can be happy every day in the Lord. The key to prevailing, powerful prayer is *abiding*.

PRAYER PRINCIPLE #2:

The ordered life brings abundant blessings.

3

A TEMPER OF THE MIND

Without faith it is impossible to please God,
because anyone who comes to him must believe that he exists and
that he rewards those who earnestly seek him.
—Hebrews 11:6

In 2020, I read a news story about a sixty-four-year-old man in France who accidentally ejected from a plane at 2,500 feet. He was on a company outing when his coworkers surprised him with a joyride on a fighter jet. His heart rate immediately skyrocketed, but he got on the plane anyway. When the plane climbed four miles above the earth's surface, the man panicked and reached for something to grab. Unfortunately, that something was the ejector seat button. He burst out of the plane. Fortunately, he parachuted to earth and landed safely.[10]

What do you reach for when life falls apart?

Some people reach for alcohol. The stress of work, economic uncertainty, relationship struggles, and an unpredictable future all cause people

10. Joshua Bote, "64-year-old man accidentally ejected himself during a surprise trip on a fighter jet," *USA Today*, accessed August 15, 2021, www.usatoday.com/story/news/world/2020/04/14/french-man-ejected-himself-during-surprise-trip-fighter-jet/2988640001.

to grab a bottle. Others reach for news. Screen time replaces quiet time or family time. People were already addicted to the Internet before the pandemic of 2020–2021. Many people reach for endless entertainment. The numbness associated with binge-watching a series or immersing oneself in a movie every night takes away valuable time from more profitable pursuits.

A fair number of people reach for anger and blame when life falls apart. They lash out at others for their troubles. Domestic violence increased dramatically during the pandemic, and women and children paid the price. There's also a heightened sense of violence through gun deaths and racial tension. The sad truth is that many people who claim to be Christian reach for the same things that non-Christians do.

What about you?

Is it possible that you have failed to grasp the greatest source of strength you could have? Is it possible that by failing to abide daily in Christ, your reach naturally goes to other things before you reach for Him in prayer?

The death and resurrection of Jesus Christ should make a real difference in your life. There's nothing more solid than knowing that God loves you with an eternal, unconditional love, and that Jesus defeated sin, death, and despair on the cross. There is nothing better to reach for when you feel afraid, alone, or anxious than the hand of Jesus. True faith in the living God can help you stand up in crisis.

> **GOD LOVES YOU WITH AN ETERNAL, UNCONDITIONAL LOVE AND SENT HIS SON TO DEFEAT SIN, DEATH, AND DESPAIR ON THE CROSS.**

The first disciples seemed fearless. How did they have such a bold faith? The truth is that they didn't always. In fact, the Gospel of Mark shows their lack of faith just after the resurrection.

In Mark 16, beginning with verse 9, there is a post-resurrection story that most scholars think was added later, likely during the late second or early third century. There are good reasons for this belief. For instance, the writing tone sounds different from the rest of Mark, and verses 9–20 introduce Mary Magdalene again as though she hasn't already been an important character in the story.

FROM DOUBT TO FAITH

But when the Bible was being complied in the fifth century, this story was included because it teaches us about the way the gospel spread throughout the world, and the miracles that came when it was proclaimed. It also gives credibility. If someone were to fabricate the resurrection—to act like it happened when it really didn't—would that person talk about how so many people doubted it? No. If they made it up, they would say that everyone believed it and the disciples were always together in bold faith.

Here's what the Scripture actually says:

> When Jesus rose early on the first day of the week, he appeared first to Mary Magdalene, out of whom he had driven seven demons. She went and told those who had been with him and who were mourning and weeping. When they heard that Jesus was alive and that she had seen him, they did not believe it. Afterward Jesus appeared in a different form to two of them while they were walking in the country. These returned and reported it to the rest; but they did not believe them either. Later Jesus appeared to the Eleven as they were eating; he rebuked them for their lack of faith and their stubborn refusal to believe those who had seen him after he had risen. He said to them, "Go into all the world and preach the gospel to all creation." (Mark 16:9–15)

Jesus rebukes them for their lack of faith and hard-heartedness. Those who had been with Him, who had followed Him for three years, really struggled to believe the resurrection. Notice that it was the *believers* who really didn't believe. Scholars think that this story was added to Mark because it was relevant to the beginning of the early church. Many people *believed* in Jesus, but they still lived with a kind of unbelief. In the everyday decisions of life, Jesus really didn't make that big of a difference.

This has been called "functional atheism." People can use the words of faith, but their actions demonstrate that their faith is really in wealth, security, safety, or convenience. Lots of people claim the name of Jesus, but they don't identify with the poor like Jesus did; instead they gravitate toward the powerful. Believers can practice unbelief as a congregation when they depend too much on money or leadership models that aren't consistent with the way Jesus formed His community.

When you don't have real faith in Christ alone, you'll reach for other things. Your life will have little power. Your mission of going into the world to proclaim the gospel will get sidetracked.

**GOD IS LOOKING FOR PEOPLE WITH GENUINE FAITH.
HE WANTS US TO REACH OUT TO HIM WHEN TIMES GET TOUGH.**

God is looking for people with genuine faith. Faith fuels the mission. Faith is the reach that allows us to fully grasp the power of Christ. Jesus wants us to have genuine faith and trust in Him. He doesn't want us to be perfect. He doesn't want us to be robots doing His will. He doesn't want us to follow a bunch of religious rules without any real faith.

Abiding in God is different. Abiding is faith in action, talking and walking with God. It's the immediate reach to God when times get tough. Jesus taught, *"If you abide in me, and my words abide in you, ask whatever you wish, and it will be done for you"* (John 15:7 ESV).

How can that possibly be true, that whatever you wish, it will be done by believing it so?

It can only happen through faith. Early in his autobiography, George Müller defined faith as "the temper of the mind in the creature which responds to every revealed perfection of the Creator." In other words, only to the degree that a creature abides in God, in sync with the Lord in all things, can one expect the promise of answered prayer to be fulfilled.

This wasn't an abstract idea to Müller as it is for so many believers. Müller said he had received fifty thousand answers to prayer over his lifetime. He prayed about big and small things. He prayed in times of plenty and in days of crisis.

Toward the end of November 1857, Müller was informed that the boiler in his first orphanage had leaked considerably. It would never make it through the frigid winter of Bristol, England.

"I felt deeply concerned for the children," Müller lamented, "especially the younger infants, not wanting them to suffer because of a lack of heat. But how were we to obtain warmth?"[11] He thought of several solutions, but none of them were satisfactory. "At last, I determined to fall entirely into the hands of God, who is very merciful and of tender compassion. I decided to have the brick chamber opened in order to see the extent of the damage and whether the boiler might be repaired to carry us through the winter."[12]

The boiler fire would have to be put out before the work could begin. Unfortunately, a second crisis arose to aggravate the first. Müller wrote:

After the day was set for the repairs, a bleak north wind set in. It began to blow either on the Thursday or Friday before the Wednesday afternoon when the fire was to be put out...What was to be done? The repairs could not be put off. I asked the Lord for two things, namely, that He would be pleased to change the north wind into a south wind, and that He would give each workman *a mind to work.*" I remembered how much Nehemiah accomplished in fifty-two days while building the walls of Jerusalem, because *"the people had a mind to work."*[13]

On Tuesday, the north wind still blew freezing air. But on Wednesday, it shifted to blow from the south, exactly as Müller had prayed. The weather was so mild that no fire was needed. When the workers learned about Müller's concern for the children, they volunteered to work through the night.

"Here, then," reported Müller, "is one of our difficulties that was overcome by prayer and faith."

11. George Müller, *Release the Power of Prayer* (New Kensington, PA: Whitaker House, 2000), 66.
12. Ibid., 67.
13. Ibid., 67–68.

The reach of faith was met by the powerful hand of God.

Müller had learned to trust God even in the darkest of days. He shows us that a crisis in circumstances doesn't have to be a crisis of faith.

What are you facing right now? Are you worried for your family? Is your health compromised? Has infertility weighed down your heart? Do you wonder how you can let go of destructive habits?

Right now, reach for God in prayer.

Remember, Jesus is alive. As you pray, He's at the right hand of your heavenly Father, interceding for you. (See Hebrews 7:25.)

He's waiting to answer you. Do you believe it?

PRAYER PRINCIPLE #3:

Faith is the reach that allows you to grasp Christ's power.

4

NO POSTMAN REQUIRED

Now to him who is able to do immeasurably more than all we ask
or imagine, according to his power that is at work within us,
to him be glory in the church and in Christ Jesus throughout all
generations, for ever and ever! Amen.
—Ephesians 3:20–21

My first pastorate was a church in rural Alabama that was mostly comprised of farmers, small business owners, and shift workers. It was a wonderful experience, God did some amazing things during those years. Although the church couldn't pay me much, they were generous in love and service.

My father became critically ill in the season I served that little church. We began to travel back and forth to Birmingham, where Dad was either hospitalized or in physical therapy. The cost of extra gas and other expenses meant money was tight. I prayed that God would supply what we needed, but I didn't know how it would come.

The Sunday after my father's diagnosis, a church member came up to me and expressed his compassion for what my dad was going through. As he shook my hand, he left a $20 bill in my palm. It was enough to get me to Birmingham and back the next day.

The following week, another person did the same thing, this time with a $50 bill. For the next eighteen months, even though I didn't get a salary increase, all that we needed was supplied in this unlikely way.

Time and time again, God has shown me that He not only provides what I need, but He provides *"exceeding abundantly above all that we ask or think"* (Ephesians 3:20 KJV)—more than what is needed. And God often does so in surprising ways.

Jesus taught us to pray for daily bread. In today's economy, that means enough money for rent, groceries, and other essentials. In Jesus's time, "daily bread" literally meant *daily bread*. Many people didn't know if they would have enough for each day.

The teaching harkens back to the time when the Israelites were completely dependent on God for manna from heaven during their wandering in the wilderness. (See Numbers 11.) It appeared like frost on the ground each morning and *"tasted like wafers made with honey"* (Exodus 16:31).

For a forty-year period between the exodus from Egypt and their entrance into the promised land, God provided food for the people every day. The catch was that they could only gather enough for one day. If they tried to store it away, *"it bred worms and stank"* (Exodus 16:20 ESV). The only exception was that they could gather twice as much on the day before the Sabbath so that they could observe the day of rest. (See Exodus 16:23–24.)

It's hard for us to understand that kind of living. We are immersed in a system in which our needs are provided for and then some. The result is that we don't really link our daily needs with the Lord. We don't pray for the little things we need, like wisdom, or the courage to speak up, or freedom from worry, or God's protection over those we love. We don't pray that others would have their daily bread.

We don't give thanks for what God gives or pause long enough to think that God may have provided more than enough for us so that we can give to others.

Could it be that our lives are filled with anxiety, frustration, and fear because we have forgotten that God is our provider? Could it be that we don't experience more of the "*immeasurably more*" promise of God because we haven't learned daily trust in the living Lord?

WE DON'T GIVE THANKS FOR WHAT GOD GIVES OR PAUSE LONG ENOUGH TO THINK THAT GOD MAY HAVE PROVIDED MORE THAN ENOUGH SO THAT WE CAN GIVE TO OTHERS.

LIVING ON THE EDGE

George Müller lived on the edge of faith regarding his finances. He dreamed a big dream of opening orphanages for thousands of children. Müller trusted in God alone to provide. He never asked anyone for donations but instead prayed, waiting on the Lord and watching for ways that God would provide.

One day, the needs of the orphanage were exceedingly great. Having nothing for the day's expenses, Müller watched the mail for a donation that could provide bread and milk for the orphans.

On March 9, 1842, Müller wrote these words in his diary:

Since our need was so great, and my soul was, through grace, truly waiting upon the Lord, I watched for supplies during the course of the morning. The mail, however, had been delivered, and no provisions had come. This did not in the least discourage me. I said to myself, "The Lord can send means without a postman. Even now, although the mail has come, through this very delivery of letters, God may have sent the answer, although the money is not yet in my hands."[14]

When the postman didn't deliver any funds, Müller continued to pray. It wasn't long before ten pounds that had been sent to another orphanage

14. Müller, *Release the Power of Prayer*, 32.

made its way to him. It was just enough for the day's expenses. God had provided the resources in a surprising way.

I love how Müller wrote that even though the funds didn't come through the mail, "This did not in the least discourage me." What faith! Müller believed that God was able to do *"immeasurably more than all we ask or imagine, according to his power that is at work within us"* (Ephesians 3:20). The funds had been provided. They were on their way. He only needed to continue in prayer.

Coincidence? Luck? If this was a one-time event, there might be reason to doubt. But Müller had similar experiences over and over and over again.

The simplest explanation is the most likely one. God hears our prayers, delights to help us, and sends aid when we need it the most.

A THREE-QUESTION CHALLENGE

Let me challenge you with three questions:

First, do you regularly acknowledge your complete reliance on God?

When George Müller prayed, he remembered that "the prayer which has been manifestly answered was the offspring of deep humility, of conscious unworthiness, of utter self-negation, and of simple and earnest reliance on the promises of God through the mediation of Christ."[15]

> *YOU WILL ONLY BE CLOSE TO GOD TO THE DEGREE THAT YOU KNOW YOUR NEEDINESS AND DEPENDENCE ON GOD'S HELP.*

You will only be close to God to the degree that you know your neediness and dependence on God's help. Power can't flow to those who don't know they need power.

Each day, you can pray, "God, I know how much I need You. I know that I am not worthy to call upon You for help, but You love me and want

---

15. Müller, *The Life of Trust*.

me to ask You for everything I need. I surrender my pride in thinking that I can do everything for myself. I trust You to supply what's required to serve You and Your kingdom today."

When you start the day like that, the blessing of God can flow from His hands to you and even through your hands to others.

Second, what specifically do you need today?

Maybe you need financial help. Maybe you need peace in a decision you're facing. Maybe you need God's help to bring home a prodigal son or daughter. Maybe you need God's assistance in keeping your business afloat. Maybe you need people to help you not be so lonely.

Don't be afraid to ask for what you need. Believe that God is able to do "*immeasurably more*" than what you ask or imagine.

Whatever our hopes and dreams are, God is always able to do more. Think of what God can do through you. Think of all that God can do in your community through your church. Now double that, triple that—multiply it by one million. That's the way God thinks. God gave you the Holy Spirit to see God's dreams become reality.

> *The Spirit of God, who raised Jesus from the dead, lives in you. And just as God raised Christ Jesus from the dead, he will give life to your mortal bodies by this same Spirit living within you.*
>
> (Romans 8:11 NLT)

God's powerful Spirit in you is the source of life, help, and hope.

Name your biggest need. Believe that God hears your prayer and that God is ready and willing to help.

Third, from where are you ultimately expecting help?

When you commit your way to the Lord, God can bring help from places you have never considered. Watch for ways that God is answering prayer. Expect help from unlikely places. The psalmist wrote:

> *I lift up my eyes to the hills. From where does my help come? My help comes from the LORD, who made heaven and earth.*
>
> (Psalm 121:1–2 ESV)

Help doesn't come from the hills, but from the Creator of the hills. Help is found not in the strength of the mountain, but in the Maker of the mountain. God makes everything, owns everything, and grants everything. Every gift you receive—whether mail, bread, or overflowing blessings—comes from the hand of the Lord, whether you acknowledge it or not.

Psalm 50:10 says the Lord owns *"the cattle on a thousand hills."* We may be finite and limited, but God has abundant, endless resources. His Word says:

> *I know every bird in the mountains, and the insects in the fields are mine…The world is mine, and all that is in it.* (Psalm 50:11–12)

God has overflowing gifts to give and a thousand delivery systems to get those resources to us. God can use the U.S. Postal Service, United Parcel Service, or Federal Express. He can use Venmo, PayPal, Zelle, or a zillion other means. God can use family, friends, strangers, and even enemies.

"Be assured," said George Müller, "if you walk with Him, and look to Him, and expect help from Him, He will never fail you."

PRAYER PRINCIPLE #4:

Watch for surprising ways that God answers prayer.

5

LEAGUE OF THE LAID LOW

Rejoice always, pray continually, give thanks in all circumstances;
for this is God's will for you in Christ Jesus.
—1 Thessalonians 5:16–18

Each Tuesday morning, I block off time to pray for the needs of our church. Even if I have a morning appointment, my goal is to pray for at least ninety minutes, but hopefully for two hours, bringing everything I can think of to God.

Sometimes distractions are hard to overcome. That's why it's important to schedule a longer block of time. My experience has been that it can often take thirty minutes or even an hour before I feel like I have made a breakthrough. God has to help my distracted, worried, and wounded heart settle down and lean into His presence. Often I begin burdened and weary but emerge energized and encouraged.

PRAYING THROUGH A TO Z

I use a prayer practice that may seem strange but that I have found to be very effective. It's praying through the alphabet. I start with A and ask the Spirit of God to bring to my mind those things for which I need to pray. First I pray for church members whose names begin with A, for God's help in reaching people in apartments, for angels to watch over our children. Then I move on to B—for more baptisms, blessings on our youth. Then comes C—college ministry. And so on.

J is an easy one because three of our main church leaders are Jaynie, Jan, and Jim. Of course, I also pray for my wife Jen. I'll admit that coming up with something for X and Z are tough. Sometimes I will think of the "X-factor" of prayer, asking God to help me bring everything before the Lord and not neglect this central, powerful gift. A friend recommended that a good prayer for Z is Zoom because so many people have struggled to use that online tool to connect with people remotely. It's a prompt to ask God to keep our church unified and mindful of those who are isolated.

> **THE PRACTICE OF PRAYING THROUGH THE ALPHABET HELPS ME ACKNOWLEDGE THAT NOTHING IS TOO BIG OR TOO SMALL FOR GOD.**

The practice of praying through the alphabet helps me acknowledge that nothing is too big or too small for God. Everything is a matter of prayer. If anything matters, everything matters.

Sometimes I'll pray for big things that seem overwhelming. I feel the burden of those prayers as I bring them again and again before God. Praying for big items especially helps me remember my complete dependence on God for all things.

The apostle Paul said that believers need to pray continually. Jesus taught His disciples that *"they should always pray and not give up"* (Luke 18:1). What else can it mean to pray always and continually if it doesn't mean in all things?

George Müller believed that the vision to open orphanages was from God. He wanted to help children in need, but more than that, he wanted to offer "visible proof" to everyday people that God still answers prayer just like God did throughout the Bible. Therefore, Müller took every need to

God. He never asked another person to supply what was lacking. Instead, he trusted that God would move people to give. He prayed for even the smallest of circumstances concerning the children's homes.

LYING LOW IN PRAYER

There was one really big point of prayer that Müller neglected. He took for granted that there would be plenty of applicants if a children's home was created.

Wrong.

When the time came to fill the first orphanage, there were no applications. Not one.

Müller wrote that this moment drove him to "lie low" before God in prayer and once again examine his motives for launching the home. Was it for his glory or God's glory?

Having discerned that indeed the vision was from God for God's glory, Müller was brought to a place of peace "that I could say from my heart that I should rejoice in God being glorified in this matter, though it were by bringing the whole to nothing."[16] In other words, Müller trusted that if after all the prayers, plans, and preparations, God purposed not to bring the home into being, he would still trust in God and rest in the belief that God would be glorified to a greater degree.

We should certainly pray specifically. We need not wonder if God wants to bring prodigal sons, daughters, or grandchildren home or if He wants to grant us victory over a temptation.

Specific prayers flow from a life that entrusts everything to God. Having brought everything before God's throne, however, we also need to learn to rest in God to work out our prayer requests in His own timing and His own way. We need to leave the outcomes in God's hands. We need to give thanks no matter what happens. Along the path of coming to God's answer, our purpose is to pray continually. God is not put off by our repeated prayers. In fact, challenges and setbacks offer another level of prayerful trust and engagement with God.

---

16. Müller, *The Life of Trust*.

As I read about this episode in Müller's life, I wondered, "Do I have enough faith to trust in God even when circumstances don't work out like I believe they should? Do I believe that in the moments when I am disappointed, God is receiving more glory than if God had granted my request?"

In a short amount of time, the first applicant arrived at the orphanage. Then a flood of applicants came such that people had to be turned away.

God must have wanted to teach Müller something. Perhaps God wanted Müller to acknowledge more fully all that He had done thus far. Perhaps God wanted to keep Müller in a state of close fellowship so that pride wouldn't enter his heart.

The prophet Habakkuk knew what it was to have faith even when a burden seemed overwhelming. He wrote:

> *Though the fig tree does not bud and there are no grapes on the vines, though the olive crop fails and the fields produce no food, though there are no sheep in the pen and no cattle in the stalls, yet I will rejoice in the LORD, I will be joyful in God my Savior.*   (Habakkuk 3:17–18)

The "laid low" will always be lifted up by the strong arm of God.

The prideful, on the other hand, can expect to be taken down a few rungs on the ladder.

Those who exalt themselves will be humbled, while the humble will be exalted. (See Luke 18:14.) This truth rests at the heart of God's kingdom.

WHEN YOU EXPERIENCE AN EXTREME HARDSHIP, FAILURE, DISAPPOINTMENT, OR DEEP NEED, THAT'S THE TIME TO BRING EVERYTHING BEFORE GOD.

When you experience an extreme hardship, failure, disappointment, or deep need, that's the time to get in your private place of prayer and bring everything before God. That's the time to lay low and seek the Lord. God will work on your heart; and when the work is done, you'll be ready for the next level. Only God can raise you to that place after a time of preparation and purification.

Do you have a regular, extended time of prayer each week?

Do you pray continually throughout the day?

Do you pray about all things?

Are you abiding in the living God so that you can *"ask whatever you wish, and it will be done for you"* (John 15:7 ESV)?

Start today.

PRAYER PRINCIPLE #5:

Because everything matters, bring everything to God in prayer.

SECTION TWO

COMPLETE DEPENDENCE
ON GOD

6

I SHALL NOT WANT

The LORD is my shepherd; I shall not want.
—Psalm 23:1 (ESV)

I've traveled on several occasions to Tanzania to help train pastors. I'm always impressed with the faith and dedication of these pastors even though they usually have much less access to resources and training than we do in the United States. They know how to pray and trust in the Good Shepherd as they are called to shepherd their churches.

Wherever I have gone in Tanzania, there have been people tending their flocks along the roadside. Some of them have had cows, but many have had sheep and goats. These shepherds, called the Maasai, carry a long staff in one hand and a spear in the other hand. They use the staff to guide the sheep and the spear to protect them against predators, such as lions and hyenas.

My hosts in Tanzania once told me that for the Maasai, their animals are everything. I learned that when the Maasai greet each other, they don't say "hello" in Swahili or another local language. Instead, they say, "I hope your animals are well."

I also learned that the Maasai don't count their sheep. Rather than accounting for their sheep by number, instead they know the details of each animal, such as its coloring, shape, size, and the unique sounds it makes. They know their animals on a deeper level. Similarly, the sheep are completely oriented toward their Maasai shepherd. The sheep trust the shepherd to supply everything they need.

"I SHALL NOT WANT"

Psalm 23 may be the most loved and best known chapter of the Bible. It is among the most quoted Scriptures because it speaks to the heart.

This psalm begins by saying that God is like a shepherd watching over the sheep, leading them to still waters and green pastures. Then the author, King David, becomes very personal, noting that the Lord "restores *my* soul. Even though *I* walk through the darkest valley, You are with me." The psalm is all about the good things God does for David: preparing a table for him, anointing him with oil, and filling his cup. David is implying, "He really does know everything about me. He knows what I need. He provides everything I need. And not just some of the time, but all of the time. He feeds me. He brings me to good places. He is totally trustworthy."

PSALM 23 HAS CONVEYED COMFORT TO MILLIONS OF PEOPLE AT FUNERALS. BUT IT'S ALSO RELATABLE TO EVERYDAY LIFE.

This psalm has conveyed comfort to millions of people at funerals. But could it be that it's not just about the end of life, but about everyday life?

Do you believe that God will supply all your needs and that there is nothing you will want for in this life?

George Müller believed it.

Sometimes, when I read about his life, I get a little discouraged. To use an analogy, if faith was a car, I would drive a Ford Model T while Müller cruised in a Lamborghini. His trust in God was a gourmet meal compared to my "fast food" faith.

I take heart in knowing that Müller was not always a person of such strong faith and stellar character. As a young boy in the 1800s, Müller often stole from his father. He was once thrown into jail for not paying a hotel bill.[17] When Müller attended Bible college, he was more likely to be found at a bar or in a back room gambling than in a Scripture study group. He also mocked Christians for their faith.

In short, Müller trusted in himself much more than in God.

LEARNING TO TRUST GOD

Once he was invited by a friend to attend an off-campus Bible study. Müller thought it would be interesting to go so that he could later make fun of the believers. However, he was surprised when he discovered that he actually enjoyed the Bible study. All of his former pleasures dwarfed in comparison to what he felt when studying God's Word and praying in the fellowship of believers. "Whether I fell on my knees when I returned home, I do not remember," Müller recounted, "but this I know, that I lay peaceful and happy in my bed."[18] He attended another Bible study the next night, and then the next. He began to be transformed by the compelling faith he saw in other believers and by their simple trust in God.

The change in his life was immediate. He stopped going to bars and mocking believers. He spent more time in worship, reading his Bible, and talking to others about God. This was the beginning of a life of faith. But there was a moment that jumpstarted his trust in the living God for all things.

When Müller told his father that he felt called to become a missionary, his father became irate. He wanted Müller to become the clergyman at a wealthy parish, not become a struggling missionary, and warned him that he would no longer pay for his schooling if he chose that path.

Müller returned to school not knowing how he would pay for his tuition. He decided to do something that many people, including Christians, might consider foolish. He got on his knees and asked God to provide. Shortly afterward, Müller was offered a paid tutoring job that was enough to cover

---

17. Müller, *The Life of Trust.*
18. Ibid.

his expenses. Müller was amazed. This was the beginning of his complete dependence on God.

Our problem is that we tend to have faith on one level, but practice life on another level. By the daily schedules we keep, the way we conduct our finances, or the way we think about careers and retirement, we can use the language of faith while our actions suggest otherwise.

You might say, "Doesn't God wants us to use common sense? Doesn't God want us to save for the future so we won't be a burden on others?"

It's certain that God wants us to be wise and good stewards of all that He has given us. The problem—or perhaps the blessing—is that we generally have more than enough. We have so much that we don't have to depend on God for daily bread or future blessing. We don't see the excess of God's gifts as being the help others may need.

In October 1856, when George Müller was advancing in years, a kind donor sent him a hundred British pounds (£100) to start a fund for his retirement. Before this offer, Müller had never saved a penny for his future. He trusted God to provide him with daily bread, praying for the needs of his family as well as the orphans under his care.

Müller recalled, "By God's grace I had not a moment's hesitation as to what to do. While I most fully appreciated the great kindness of the donor, I looked upon this as being permitted by God as a temptation to put my trust in something else than himself."[19]

In his return letter to the donor, Müller wrote:

I have no property whatever, nor has my dear wife; nor have I had one single shilling regular salary as a minister of the gospel for the last twenty-six years, nor as the director of the Orphan House and the other objects of the Scriptural Knowledge Institution for Home and Abroad. When I am in need of anything, I fall on my knees, and ask God that he would be pleased to give me what I need; and he puts it into the heart of some one or another to help me. Thus all my wants have been amply supplied during the last twenty-six years, and I can say, to the praise of God, I have lacked nothing... Of this blessed way of living none of us are tired, but become day by

---

19. Müller, *The Life of Trust.*

day more convinced of its blessedness…Under these circumstances, I am unable to accept your kindness of the gift of one hundred pounds towards making a provision for myself and family.[20]

After receiving Müller's letter and understanding his heart, the donor replied back that he would be pleased if Müller used the money for the orphans. Then the donor sent another hundred pounds…and later another hundred.

Can you imagine living that way? How would your life be different if the words of Psalm 23:1 became a true and practical expression of your faith?

I can't answer that question for you. You can't answer it for me. All I know is that I look at my life and find myself ashamed of my lack of trust for daily bread and future needs.

God, help me. God, help us all.

GEORGE MÜLLER WASN'T ALWAYS A MAN OF GREAT FAITH. GOD CHANGED HIS HEART. MAYBE IT'S NOT TOO LATE FOR YOU AND ME.

I take heart in knowing that Müller wasn't always a man of great faith. God changed his heart. Maybe it's not too late for you and me.

Maybe with the time you and I have left, we could learn to be more generous. We could stop chasing possessions. We could let go of some of our dreams that essentially keep others from receiving a blessing of God through our hands. We could plan for retirement differently. We could fall on our knees more and ask God to provide for us so that we could spend God's money in God's way.

It's not too late to trust the Good Shepherd.

BELIEVING THE TRUTH OF PSALM 23

There's an old story, likely apocryphal, from the 1800s. It was a time before entertainment through movies and television. People instead

_____

20. Müller, *The Life of Trust*.

gathered to hear great orators and storytellers. On one such occasion, a well-known actor with a dynamic voice traveled to a small town. The town hall was packed. After his recitation of poems, the thrilled audience was invited to make some requests.

A frail, elderly man with a weathered face timidly raised his hand and asked, "Would you please recite the Twenty-Third Psalm?"

The actor agreed on one condition: that after he finished, the elderly man would rise and also recite the psalm.

The orator began, "The Lord is my shepherd" with great drama and diction. He infused the words with a weight and cadence, moving the people to imagine deep valleys of shadows and tables set before enemies. It was powerful. As he concluded, the people rose to their feet with a standing ovation.

Then the man who requested the psalm arose. He wasn't handsome, well-dressed, or eloquent. But as he began to speak, his voice thick with belief and emotion, a hush fell over the crowd. His face took on a glow of joy.

When he finished with the words, *"Surely goodness and mercy shall follow me all the days of my life, and I shall dwell in house of the* LORD *forever"* (Psalm 23:6 ESV), the only sound in the room was the rustle of handkerchiefs as the crowd brushed away tears.

The silence was broken only when the actor spoke again. "Now you know why I wanted him to follow me, not the other way around," he said. "You see, I know the psalm, but he—he knows the Shepherd."

Is it personal for you? Do you know that God knows you intimately, including your every need?

Pray the first line of Psalm 23 from your heart today. Pray it until the truth of it sinks into your soul.

Let God lead you to the still waters and green pastures. Ask God to restore your soul today.

PRAYER PRINCIPLE #6:

When you let the Good Shepherd lead you, you'll want for nothing.

7

CLOSET COMMUNION

Be still, and know that I am God;
I will be exalted among the nations, I will be exalted in the earth.
—Psalm 46:10

In 2010, I traveled with a group of pastors to South Korea to learn from other pastors. South Korea is home to some of the world's largest churches. Our group of pastors wanted to know how the South Korean churches multiplied disciples and groups with such success.

In the United States, a church with 10,000 or 15,000 members is considered extremely large, but amazingly, South Korean churches can sometimes have 50,000 or even half a million members.

The Yoido Full Gospel Church, founded by David Yonggi Cho, had over 800,000 members when I worshipped there in 2010.

Pastor Cho was constantly asked about his secret for church growth. On such occasions, he often gave a surprising answer. He would lift three fingers. Counting one finger down at a time, he would say, "First, prayer. Second, prayer. Third, prayer. That's it!"[21]

---

21. Robert Oh, *The Prayer Driven Life* (e-edition), accessed August 15, 2021, www.christianinternationalchurch.org/wp-content/uploads/2016/01/ThePDL.pdf.

One might think that Pastor Cho had little time to pray each day. It was widely known, however, that he prayed two to three hours daily. Given all that the Lord had placed in his hands, he reasoned that he must pray longer and longer for wisdom and help.

THE HEARTBEAT OF BELIEVERS

Prayer is never a vehicle for church growth. It's not a tool in the toolbox. Rather, it is part of the DNA of any healthy, thriving church. It must be the heartbeat of every true believer.

Whether God has placed little or much in your hands to manage, all followers of Jesus need to spend time every day in stillness, remember that God is God, and seek wisdom and help.

> **ALL FOLLOWERS OF JESUS NEED TO SPEND TIME EVERY DAY IN STILLNESS, REMEMBER THAT GOD IS GOD, AND SEEK WISDOM AND HELP.**

One paradox of faith is that one's busyness *for* the Lord can actually take one away *from* the Lord.

Early in his ministry in Bristol, England, George Müller identified this tendency in his own life.

He journaled on April 21, 1832:

Often the work of the Lord itself may be a temptation to keep us from that communion with him which is so essential to the benefit of our own souls. On the 19th I had left Dartmouth, conversed a good deal that day, preached in the evening, walked afterwards eight miles, had only about five hours' sleep, travelled again the next day twenty-five miles, preached twice, and conversed very much besides, went to bed at eleven, and arose before five. All this shows that my body and spirit required rest, and, therefore, however careless about the Lord's work I might have appeared to my brethren, I ought to have had a great deal of quiet time for prayer and reading the word, especially as I had a long journey before me that day...Instead of this, I hurried to the prayer meeting, after a few minutes' private prayer. But let none think that public prayer will make up for closet communion. Then again, afterwards, when I ought to have withdrawn myself, as it were, by force, from the company of beloved brethren and sisters, and given my testimony for the Lord...by telling them that I needed secret communion with the Lord, I did not do so, but spent the time, till the coach came, in conversation with them.[22]

Müller was pouring out his life for the Lord. Like any other activity, however, his religious pursuits squeezed out essential time in the private presence of Jesus.

This has happened to me more than I care to admit. After twenty-five years of ministry, busyness still tempts me. The danger is that I develop a pretense of devotion and serving. My heart can be far from the Lord in those moments. I have discovered that sometimes I can inadvertently lead people *away from* Jesus rather than *toward* Him even though what I am doing seems very devout. I demonstrate in those times that busyness matters more than the heart.

That's also what Müller felt after he left the assembly of brothers and sisters. He lamented, "My own soul needed food; and not having had it, I was lean, and felt the effects of it the whole day; and hence I believe it came that I was dumb on the coach, and did not speak a word for Christ, nor give away a single tract, though I had my pockets full on purpose."[23]

Spending too much time on good things can cause you to miss the best things.

How much has God placed in your hands?

In this book's introductory chapter, I told the story of a ship's captain, a prayer from the chartroom, and a fog that was miraculously lifted.

---

22. Müller, *The Life of Trust*.
23. Ibid.

PUTTING GOD FIRST

Each of us is a kind of captain. We all have God-given responsibilities. There are relationships, tasks, and opportunities that God places in your hands and mine.

Apart from a deep, abiding relationship in the Lord and the presence of the Holy Spirit, you and I won't manage those responsibilities very well. We may look busy for the Lord, but we'll miss the chance to share our faith or give a cup of cold water in Jesus's name.

Most of all, we will miss the gift of secret communion with our heavenly Father.

God said, "*I will be exalted among the nations, I will be exalted in the earth*" (Psalm 46:10). In other words, it will happen apart from your most frantic efforts. Jesus said, "*I will build my church, and the gates of Hades will not overcome it*" (Matthew 16:18).

Jesus never said to me, "Brent, you're responsible to build My church. I'm counting on your strength, your brains, and your sacrificial efforts." Jesus is the one who builds the church. He sets the vision, supplies the power, and gives the increase. That way, He receives all the glory.

So, what is our role? Yes, we are called to serve with diligence and hard work. I agree with John Wesley who said, "Do all that you can, by all the means you can, in all the ways you can, in all the places you can, at all the times you can, to all the people you can, as long as you ever can." One day, we want to hear the words, "*Well done, good and faithful servant*" (Matthew 25:23). There is a big difference between those who talk and those who do.

But we also must recognize that we can't change people's hearts. We can't make any impact apart from God's help. We may do our part, but God does the heavy lifting.

WE CAN'T CHANGE PEOPLE'S HEARTS.
WE CAN'T MAKE ANY IMPACT APART FROM GOD'S HELP.
WE MAY DO OUR PART, BUT GOD DOES THE HEAVY LIFTING.

What we *must* do is stay close to the heart of our heavenly Father. We must be shaped in prayer. We must be conformed to the image of Christ. If ever we neglect this sacred work, then we surely will be pursuing our own kingdom rather than the kingdom of Jesus Christ. We'll soon reap the results of worrisome days, frenetic busyness, and undirected action.

The more God has given you to manage, the more time you need to *be still* in prayer.

Only then can God show you what you can never see through your own strength.

FINDING AMAZING GRACE

When Fred Craddock was a boy, he lived on a farm adjacent to an older neighbor named Will. Six-year-old Fred asked the man, who was in his eighties, "Mr. Will, have you ever been in a church?"

Will replied, "In a church? All the time I'm in a church."

Fred said, "I mean do you go to church?"

"I go every Sunday," the gentleman replied.

"Really," Fred asked. "What's it like?"

His neighbor said, "You wouldn't believe what it's like. When I walk up to that golden door and touch that silver handle and open the door, well a hundred voices say, 'Welcome, Will!' I go in, and there must be five hundred in the choir. And the ceiling of that building is blue like the ceiling of heaven, with stars sprinkled throughout. And everyone is singing, including the angels. It is absolutely unbelievable. Do I go to church? Of course I go to church!"

Fred went to Will's church once. It was an unpainted, clapboard frame building that seated about sixty. The seats were handmade and worn down.

Fred said he didn't realize until much later that Will could see what he couldn't see—that sometimes God disguises the good stuff. You have to adjust your eyes and lay down your expectations to see it. You have to be still.

A few years later, Mr. Will passed away. Young Fred and his family went to the funeral in that little, unassuming church God had placed in the backwoods. When the service started, however, something strange happened. The choir began singing and swaying. The congregation joined in. And suddenly, Fred looked up.

"And do you know? The ceiling was blue. And the stars were shining all about. And ministries of angels sang Will to his rest."[24]

It may be that the greatest triumph of a person's faith is not in accomplishing a great task for God, bringing many souls to Christ, or selling all that person has for the kingdom of God. The greatest triumph may come when a person learns to simply be still—content, ready, and trusting—in the presence of the Almighty.

From that place of stillness, God can grow a church. God can move mountains.

How does this truth intersect your life? What do you need to do in response?

Ask God to help you spend the time you need in prayer and communion.

Seek God's help in reordering your days to put God first.

Be still.

PRAYER PRINCIPLE #7:

The more God gives you to manage, the more time you need in prayer.

24. Jessica Hartman, "Giving Up Expectations, A Sermon by Alan Sherouse," from "Fred Craddock at Festival of Homiletics, May 2007," accessed August 15, 2021, fbcgso.org/giving-up-expectations-a-sermon-by-alan-sherouse.

8

SEVEN HUNDRED
AND TWENTY-NINE SOULS

Revive us so we can call on your name once more.
—Psalm 80:18 (NLT)

I once witnessed a strange Easter parade. This one didn't have floats, children in new spring clothes, colorful eggs, or candy. But I believe it was the type of parade that would have made Jesus smile on that Easter Sunday.

As I was on my way to enter our sanctuary in Dallas, I watched as a group of men and women walked single-file through the doors of the church. I had never seen them before, but I soon learned that they were from a local recovery center. That Easter morning, a staff member had decided he wanted to attend a worship service even though he was working. He asked permission to take anyone from the recovery program who wanted to go.

Little did he know that sixty men and women were going to sign up.

Through the detox and treatment program, these women and men were seeking a new start. While their lives were often a train wreck, one good thing was that their hearts were receptive to God's voice.

A PARADE OF NEW BELIEVERS

That Easter Sunday was the beginning of a two-year blessing for our church. Each Sunday, the single-file train of men and women walked three blocks to our church building. Many people came to the altar at the end of each service, praying for help, hope, and healing. They prayed for their families, confessing shame and sorrow for how they had treated the people closest to them. Each week, someone new wanted to be baptized. Believing that more and more people would turn to Christ, we kept the baptistery full of water.

Soon we started a Bible study called "Storytellers," centered on the stories Jesus told. The format was simple. Someone would tell a Bible story, such as the Lord meeting the Samaritan woman at the well in John 4, and then group members were asked to repeat what they heard in the story. It was so refreshing to watch people's reactions upon hearing a Bible story for the first time.

The stories of faith in God's Word became living stories to first-time listeners.

For over two years, we saw lives changing before our eyes. That Easter morning procession developed into a steady stream of baptisms among dozens and dozens of new believers.

It could only be called a revival.

Have you ever experienced anything like that? I can testify that watching that revival unfold strengthened my faith, renewed my belief in the power of the gospel to save, and made me a better proclaimer of the message of Jesus Christ.

> **WATCHING A CHURCH REVIVAL UNFOLD STRENGTHENED MY FAITH AND RENEWED MY BELIEF IN THE POWER OF THE GOSPEL TO SAVE.**

The children under George Müller's care received food, shelter, education, and apprenticeship in various trades. They also received spiritual nourishment but were never pressured to accept faith in Jesus Christ. Though prayer, Bible study, and spiritual counsel, however, many children experienced God's love and salvation through Müller's ministry.

A REVIVAL FOR THE ORPHANS

In some seasons, Müller and his fellow workers would pray for revival to come to the orphan homes.

Müller recounts that in the years 1871–1872:

> The spiritual condition of the Orphans generally gave to us great sorrow of heart, because there were so few, comparatively, among them, who were in earnest about their souls, and resting on the atoning death of the Lord Jesus for salvation. This our sorrow led us to lay it on the whole staff of assistants, matrons and teachers, to seek earnestly the Lord's blessing on the souls of the children.[25]

Imagine the whole operation of workers praying for the children. They prayed in special meetings. They prayed in secret. They prayed *earnestly*. Then God began to move earnestly.

Unfortunately, that movement happened in the midst of a smallpox outbreak.

Müller wrote:

> On Jan. 8, 1872, the Lord began to work among them, and this work was going on more or less afterwards. In the New Orphan-House No. 3, it showed itself least, till it pleased the Lord to lay His hand heavily on that house, by the small-pox; and, from that time the working of the Holy Spirit was felt in that house also, particularly in one department. At the end of July, 1872, I received the statements of all the matrons and teachers in the five houses, who reported to me, that, after careful observation and conversation, they had good reason to believe that 729 of the Orphans then under our care, were believers in the Lord Jesus. This number of believing Orphans is by far greater than ever we had, for which we

---

25. George Mueller, *Answers to Prayer: From George Mueller's Narratives Compiled by A. E. C. Brooks* (Chicago: Moody Publishers, 2007), 84.

adore and praise the Lord! See how the Lord overruled the great trial, occasioned by the small-pox, and turned it into a great blessing! See, also, how, after so low a state, comparatively, which led us to prayer, earnest prayer, the working of the Holy Spirit was more manifest than ever![26]

Through his eyes of faith, Müller saw that God had nullified the suffering from smallpox as children turned to God for help. Through this great trial, everyone called on the name of the Lord.

By grace, sometimes God will put you in a place where you *must* pray.

That's where the men and women in recovery found themselves. It was true of the children and workers at Müller's orphanage.

It was also true of the first family.

After Adam and Eve's sin, humankind quickly started to descend into chaos. Shame came over the first human family. Their sons, Cain and Abel, got into a bitter dispute. Cain killed Abel. Apart from God, humans were spiraling out of control.

The Bible says:

Adam made love to his wife again, and she gave birth to a son and named him Seth, saying, "God has granted me another child in place of Abel, since Cain killed him." Seth also had a son, and he named him Enosh. **At that time people began to call on the name of the Lord.**

(Genesis 4:25–26)

This happened before anyone was called a *Hebrew* or a *Christian*. This was before Moses, Abraham, and the prophets. It was before Jesus walked the earth. The journey of humanity back to God began with people learning to call on the name of the Lord.

THE JOURNEY OF HUMANITY BACK TO GOD BEGAN WITH PEOPLE LEARNING TO CALL ON THE NAME OF THE LORD.

---

26. Mueller, *Answers to Prayer*, 84–85.

The word *call* means to cry out or implore for aid. This is the heart of prayer that reaches the ears of God.

God said through the prophet Jeremiah, *"Call to me and I will answer you and tell you great and unsearchable things you do not know"* (Jeremiah 33:3). God wants us to call out from the depths of our hearts to the heights of heaven. From God's throne, God shares wisdom and knowledge about secret things.

This is where revival begins.

Whether it was the Great Awakening, the Second Great Awakening, the Welsh Revival, or the Azusa Street Revival, revival begins when men and women cry out to God with broken hearts and yearn for change in their lives and their communities.

In Psalm 80, the writer Asaph groans about the awful state of his people. The walls have been broken down. Wild animals run through the streets. The vines have been chopped down. Finally, Asaph calls out, *"Revive us so we can call on your name once more"* (Psalm 80:18 NLT). Another translation (ESV) says, *"Give us life."*

WE ALL NEED REVIVAL

Before any person or any church can call upon the name of the Lord, there must be revival. There must be some life, a quickening of the soul. This is the work that only the Holy Spirit can do.

Revival can only come to those who have been *revived* first by God. There must be a stirring in what God has already created so that people are enabled to again call upon the name of the Lord.

Do you want to see a revival happen in your church? Do you want a revival to begin in your own soul?

All of us need a fresh stirring. We need a new encounter with the Holy Spirit. Then, we can call on the name of the Lord.

When I stand before the Lord, I believe that Jesus won't ask, "Brent, did you preach rousing, entertaining sermons? Did you write lots of books about Me?" Instead, I believe He will ask, "Did you pour your heart into helping men and women call upon My name? Did you lead people to pray?"

IT'S NEVER TOO LATE TO PRAY

In his book *Fresh Wind, Fresh Fire*, Pastor Jim Cymbala writes about his oldest daughter, Chrissy. She was a model child growing up, but around the time she turned sixteen, she started to drift away from God. The Cymbalas often wondered where their daughter was.

As the situation worsened and Chrissy fell prey to bad influences, Jim tried everything. He begged with her, argued, and tried to control her with money. Nothing worked. The Cymbalas thought about leaving New York to allow their daughter to have a less tempting environment.

One pastor counseled Jim that he should stop trying so hard, that Chrissy was going to do what she wanted to do and he should resign himself to that fact. Jim refused to believe it. He committed to pray more earnestly and only talked with God about it, no one else. He believed that God could reach down and change Chrissy's heart.

For months, he waited and waited with a broken heart. Finally, one Tuesday night at the Brooklyn Tabernacle's prayer meeting, an usher handed Jim a note. A young woman had written, "Pastor Cymbala, I feel impressed that we should stop the meeting and all pray for your daughter."

Although Cymbala had only told a few people about what was going on, he then felt led to share his heart with the congregation. "The truth of the matter," he said, "is that although I haven't talked much about it, my daughter is very far from God these days. She thinks up is down and down is up; dark is light and light is dark. But I know God can break through to her, and so I'm going to ask Pastor (Carlo) Boekstaaf to lead us in prayer for Chrissy. Let's all join hands across the sanctuary."

The prayer room became a labor room. People cried out to the Lord for Chrissy with a groaning that said, "Satan will not have this girl."

Thirty-two hours later, as Jim was shaving, his wife Carol shouted, "Go downstairs! Chrissy's here! It's you she wanted to see!"

He found his daughter sobbing on the kitchen floor. "Daddy, Daddy," she said, "I've sinned against God. I've sinned against myself. I've sinned against you and Mommy. Please forgive me." Then she abruptly drew back and said, "Who was praying for me? Who was praying for me?"

He asked, "What do you mean, Chrissy?"

"On Tuesday night, Daddy—who was praying for me? In the middle of the night, God woke me up and showed me I was heading toward this abyss. There was no bottom to it—it scared me to death. I was so frightened. I realized how hard I've been, how wrong, how rebellious. But at the same time, it was like God wrapped His arms around me and held me tight. He kept me from sliding any farther as He said, 'I still love you!' Who was praying for me Tuesday night?"[27]

Let's believe that there's great power in prayer. Let's pray for our own souls. Let's pray for the lost. Let's call out to God with a yearning like we never have had before.

Let's pray for a parade to run through the middle of our lives and churches as God does what only God can do.

Dear Lord, revive us so we can call on Your name once more.

PRAYER PRINCIPLE #8:

Sometimes God puts you in a place where you must pray.

27. Jim Cymbala, *Fresh Wind, Fresh Fire* (Grand Rapids, MI: Zondervan, 1997), 60–65.

9

IN GOD WE TRUST

Trust in the LORD with all your heart and lean not on your own
understanding; in all your ways submit to him,
and he will make your paths straight.
—Proverbs 3:5–6

Billy Graham was once in a small town and needed directions to the post office. After a boy told him how to get there, Graham invited the youth to his crusade that evening. "You can hear me telling everyone how to get to heaven," he told the boy. But the lad declined, saying, "You don't even know your way to the post office."[28]

In whom do you put your trust?

Most people get help from family members, friends, pastors, counselors, financial advisors, or neighbors. They trust these people to point them in the right direction. You may have such acquaintances.

You also may place some measure of trust in your financial situation, education, career success, or life experience. It's not wrong to pursue these

---

28. Billy Graham Evangelistic Association, "The Lighter Side of Billy Graham," accessed August 15, 2021, billygraham.org/story/the-lighter-side-of-billy-graham.

things and to seek the help of others. The problem comes when you begin to lean on these things in a way that diverts you from your trust in God.

When God began to expand the work of George Müller's orphanages, Müller remained committed to trusting in God for everything. For the first seventeen years, the largest donation Müller received was one hundred pounds (about $16,000 in today's money). That may seem like a lot, but several hundred orphans were under his care each year. He never asked people for money. Faith in the living God and prayer were his only strategies.

Müller wrote, "The Lord was pleased greatly to encourage me and to increase my faith by a donation of five hundred pounds for the orphans; for up to that period I had never received more than one hundred pounds at once."[29]

It was a huge blessing. In giving the gift, the donor suggested that Müller invest the sum and use only the interest from it. His reasoning was that there was no way the orphan institutions could be supported into the future without having some funds, property, or other resources stored up.

TRUST IN THE LIVING GOD

At that time, in 1850, Müller only operated two orphanages. Because the donor was merely making a suggestion, Müller took the money and applied it to a third house to be able to receive thirty more orphans.

Reflecting back on that season of ministry and step of faith, Müller reported:

From that time the work has been increasing more and more... Now, suppose I had said, seventeen years ago, looking at matters according to natural reason, "The two charity schools are enough, I must not go any further," then the work would have stopped there. Or, if I had a little more trust in my exertions or my friends, I might have taken at the utmost one or two steps further. Instead of this, however, I looked in no degree whatever at things according to my natural fallen reason, and I trusted not in the circle of my Christian friends, but in the living God; and the result has been that there have been since 1834 ten thousand souls under

29. Müller, *The Life of Trust*.

our instruction in the various day schools, Sunday schools, and adult schools; several hundred orphans have been brought up… several hundred thousand tracts and many thousand copies of the Word of God have been circulated…and a house has been built and fitted up for the accommodation of three hundred destitute orphans, each of whom has neither father or mother. How blessed therefore it is to trust in God, and in him alone, and not in circumstances nor friends![30]

Müller's life is a picture of faith. This is what real trust looks like. It doesn't mean Müller's choices would be the same as yours, but you can't deny that he really did put his faith in God for everyday needs and the future expansion of his ministry.

> GEORGE MÜLLER REALLY DID PUT HIS FAITH IN GOD FOR EVERYDAY NEEDS AND THE FUTURE EXPANSION OF HIS MINISTRY. THAT'S WHAT REAL TRUST LOOKS LIKE.

Müller trusted in and modeled his life on Jesus. Jesus also trusted in His heavenly Father. In his classic devotion *My Utmost for His Highest*, Oswald Chambers wrote:

Our Lord trusted no man; yet He was never suspicious, never bitter, never in despair about any man, because He put God first in trust; He trusted absolutely in what God's grace could do for any man. If I put my trust in human beings first, I will end in despairing of everyone; I will become bitter, because I have insisted on man being what no man ever can be—absolutely right. Never trust anything but the grace of God in yourself or in anyone else.[31]

Faith is leaning your full weight on Jesus, not a portion of it. I have leaned for far too long on my own understanding and natural gifts. I have

30. Müller, *The Life of Trust*.
31. Oswald Chambers, "God First," from the online edition of *My Utmost for His Highest*, accessed August 15, 2021, utmost.org/classic/god-first-classic.

trusted people when I should have trusted God. In some ways, I wasn't even aware that I was trusting too much in others and things. My anxiety, however, has revealed a heart that leans too much on temporary and imperfect things rather than trusting in the eternal, absolute character of God.

> **RATHER THAN LEANING ON TEMPORARY AND IMPERFECT THINGS, WE NEED TO TRUST IN THE ETERNAL, ABSOLUTE CHARACTER OF GOD.**

I want to live differently. I've asked God to reveal ways that I am trusting too much in the flesh rather than depending on God. I've made a list. Every now and then, I review that list and consider what God has done through His Spirit to help me trust Him more. I also realize how many areas are lacking in trust in the living God.

THREE DIRECTIONS AND ONE PROMISE

Proverbs 3:5–6 describes three urgent directions to follow and one amazing promise:

+ *"Trust in the LORD with all your heart."* Ask God to give you a deeper and abiding trust in Him. Ask God to reveal ways that you are trusting in things and people. God desires that you would trust Him with all of your heart—your emotions, your will, and your passions.

+ *"Lean not on your own understanding."* You are finite, while God is infinite. What keeps you from seeking the counsel of God and trusting when times are uncertain? Seek daily the understanding of Scripture. Seek daily the wisdom of the Holy Spirit.

+ *"In all your ways acknowledge him"* (ESV). Make sure you thank Him for everything you have. Thank God for grace. You didn't deserve any of it, but God has given it nonetheless. Be conscious of the presence of God when you go through the valley. Just speak to Him. Submit to Him. Ask Him for help.

+ *"He will make your paths straight."* What a promise. Not easy. Not short. Straight. The right path for your life. Those who trust in God will be shown the right path.

Casey Diaz tells his life story in a book called *The Shot Caller*. Diaz was in a gang in South Central Los Angeles and eventually was sentenced to thirteen years in prison for second-degree murder. In Pitchess Detention Center, Diaz was approached about being the "shot caller"—the one who called the shots. He made decisions for his gang about who got knives and who got attacked. He marked people for death.

When Casey was transferred to another prison, a guard told him they knew he was a shot caller, so they were putting him in solitary confinement, an eight-by-ten-foot windowless room. Casey had no TV, radio, or books. He only knew the passage of time when meals came.

After about a year, he heard the guards come by his cell and announce, "Protestant service. Any inmate wanting to go, stand by your gate." Diaz didn't want religion. He knew nothing about Jesus.

"JESUS IS GOING TO USE YOU"

One time he was lying on his bed when he heard the voice of an older woman outside. "Is there someone in that cell?" she asked. She sounded Southern and spoke with a syrupy drawl.

"Yes, ma'am," the guard said, "but you don't want to deal with Diaz. You're wasting your time."

"Well," she said, "Jesus came for him, too."

She asked Casey, "How are you doing?"

"I couldn't be better," he replied sarcastically.

"Young man," she said, "I'm going to pray for you. But there's something else I want to tell you: Jesus is going to use you." By then, he was certain she was crazy. After all, he was locked away in solitary confinement. But she persisted. "Young man, every time I'm here, I'm going to come by and remind you that Jesus is going to use you."

About a year later, Casey was lying in his cell when he had a vision of himself as a young child, walking in his old neighborhood in Los Angeles. He also saw scenes from his early days with a gang.

Then he saw a bearded man with long hair carrying a cross. As he trudged along, a mob of angry people shouted at him. The man was nailed to a cross, which was then raised between two other men on crosses. He looked down at Casey and said, "Darwin, I'm doing this for you."

Casey shuddered. Apart from the guards and his family, no one knew his real name. When he heard the sound of breath leaving the man on the cross, Casey started to weep because he realized that this vision could only have come from the Almighty. Even though he didn't understand what Jesus had done for him in that deepest, darkest place, he got on his knees and started confessing his sins: "God, I'm sorry for stabbing so many people. God, I'm sorry I robbed so many families." With each confession, he felt another weight come off his shoulders.

When he finished, he knew something had changed. He spoke with a chaplain who explained the gospel. Casey accepted Christ as Savior. He was beaten for his faith when he got out of solitary confinement, and his former friends abandoned him. Rather than being a shot caller, God gave Casey a new calling: telling other inmates about Jesus.[32]

He learned to trust in the living God, who made a better path for him.

Imprinted on American currency are the words "In God We Trust."

Do you trust Him?

Trust Him today. Pour out your heart. Confess your sins. Tell God that you want to trust Him with everything.

PRAYER PRINCIPLE #9:

God can be trusted more than circumstances or friends.

---

32. Casey Diaz, "I Marked People for Death. Jesus Marked Me for Life," *Christianity Today*, accessed August 15, 2021, www.christianitytoday.com/ct/2019/may/casey-diaz-shot-caller-marked-people-death-gang-leader.html.

10

A REFUGE IN
THE DAY OF TROUBLE

I call upon the LORD, *who is worthy to be praised,*
and I am saved from my enemies…In my distress I called upon the
LORD; *to my God I cried for help. From his temple he heard my*
voice, and my cry to him reached his ears.
—Psalm 18:3, 6 (ESV)

For four decades, Ramon Gonzalez ran a small barbershop on Jefferson Avenue in the heart of Oak Cliff in Dallas, Texas. He was a gentle, humble man who remarkably worked not only in the same shop but in the same spot all those years. I loved going to see him because I knew I would get more than a good haircut. I would also receive some wisdom and encouragement.

A few years after I started visiting Ramon for a haircut, he sold his business but kept working there. Then it sold again. Ramon kept cutting hair, same spot. He didn't like how the new owners ran things, but he often spoke of his faith in the Lord and how God was helping him stay steady.

One afternoon I was getting a haircut when a man came through the back door. He was screaming and cursing, out of his mind.

He made his way to the front of the shop, where the new owner was cutting hair. It turns out that the irate man had been fired that morning. Now he was back and threatening to kill the owner.

"Ramon, we need to call the police," I said. "This could escalate."

"No, he'll leave. Let's just wait and see," Ramon responded.

I wasn't convinced. Truthfully, I felt afraid. So I asked for the phone and called the police. Looking back, it was surreal to be talking to the 911 operator while Ramon calmly continued to cut my hair.

The deranged guy finally left. Everyone breathed a sigh of relief. The police showed up and said to call them again if the man returned. I paid Ramon and went home.

A few hours later, I was having dinner at a neighborhood cafe when I heard helicopters overhead. I immediately thought of the barbershop.

Charles Dewayne Hooks is now in jail for the murder of his former boss, Alejandro Fernandez. Fifteen minutes after I left, he returned and shot the owner in front of everyone.

I felt like God had protected me and others, including my friend Ramon. Amazingly, Ramon said that he had not been afraid as he witnessed this violent crime. He knew that God was his protector.

David, the shepherd boy who would become a king, also knew that his protection came from God. He wrote Psalm 18 in response to the time when King Saul was out of his mind and determined to kill David and his companions. Thus, David went into hiding, possibly in a desert cave close to his hometown of Bethlehem.

Apart from his epic failure with Bathsheba, David was in the lowest moment of his life. Away from everything he knew and everything he depended on, he felt all alone.

Revealing his heart, David wrote:

I cry aloud to the LORD; I lift up my voice to the LORD for mercy. I pour out before him my complaint; before him I tell my trouble...Look and see, there is no one at my right hand; no one is concerned for me. I have no refuge; no one cares for my life. (Psalm 142:1–2, 4)

But there was One who did care for David's life. God.

In November 1847, George Müller had an experience that he would describe as "a most remarkable deliverance" and a testimony of how God watches over His children. He described the experience as follows:

> I was laboring for a little while at Bowness and Keswick in the ministry of the word, in October and November. When at Keswick, I stayed with my dear wife in a large boardinghouse, in which, however, we were then alone, except a single gentleman. Just before we left Keswick, on the morning of Nov. 24, I heard that the gentleman, lodging in the same house, had shot himself during the night, but was not quite dead. We had not heard the report of the pistol, it being a very stormy night and the house large.[33]

Müller and his wife left the boardinghouse and later received word that the fellow boarder had been "quite deranged" for two or three days. A Christian brother wrote:

> Without any control, he had been walking about his room for the last two days and nights, with loaded pistols in his hands. Furthermore, he had taken into his head that you were going to kill him. How gracious of God that he spread his wings over you, and over dear Mrs. Müller, so that Satan could not break through the fence, to hurt even a hair on your heads…What a scene his room presented; pistols lying in gore; bloody knives, lancets, and razors strewed about the floor.[34]

God protected the Müllers even though they had no idea of the danger just around the corner.

THE BIBLE SAYS AGAIN AND AGAIN THAT GOD IS A DELIVERER FROM ENEMIES, BOTH SEEN AND UNSEEN.

---

33. Müller, *The Life of Trust.*
34. Ibid.

The Bible says again and again that God is a deliverer from enemies, both seen and unseen. God delivered Daniel from the jaws of lions, Israel from the Egyptians' pursuing chariots, Jehoshaphat from three attacking armies, and David from the hand of Saul.

Second Samuel 22:2–4 records David's celebration of praise when the threat of Saul was neutralized:

> The LORD is my rock, my fortress and my deliverer; my God is my rock, in whom I take refuge, my shield and the horn of my salvation. He is my stronghold, my refuge and my savior—from violent people you save me. I called to the LORD, who is worthy of praise, and have been saved from my enemies.

What do you do when trouble comes? Do you flail about, trying to get out of your problem? Do you freeze with fear? Do you fight with a frenzy?

When trouble came, David turned toward God.

CRYING OUT TO GOD

Here's what you can do to receive God's protection from seen and unseen enemies.

First, *cry out for your deliverance.* Ask for help from the living God. Believe that God is *"mighty to save"* (Isaiah 63:1).

Second, *wait for your deliverance.* The greatest triumph of your faith is not the big moment when God delivers you out of your worst circumstance. It's not when you accomplish some great feat for God or when you come to the culmination of your life, achieving some great purpose.

The greatest triumph of your faith is when you to come to the place of being still and knowing that God is God. *"He says, 'Be still, and know that I am God; I will be exalted among the nations, I will be exalted in the earth'"* (Psalm 46:10).

Even when the enemy surrounds you, when violent men threaten you, or when things look dark and hopeless, be still.

Corrie ten Boom observed, "When a train goes through a tunnel and it gets dark, you don't throw away the ticket and jump off. You sit still and trust the engineer."

Finally, *celebrate your deliverance*. Don't neglect to give God praise, privately and publicly, for what He has done for you. Your greatest test becomes your testimony. Your deliverance becomes your declaration.

PRAYER PRINCIPLE #10:

When trouble comes, trust God to deliver you.

11

ALL THE TIME

For I know the plans I have for you, declares the Lord, plans for
welfare and not for evil, to give you a future and a hope. Then you
will call upon me and come and pray to me, and I will hear you.
—Jeremiah 29:11–12 (esv)

My friend Wesley pastors a church in Fort Worth, Texas. For many years, Wesley took teams down to Haiti for mission work. There he met a pastor named Alphonso. Around 1980, Alphonso started his church with a grand vision of seeing many adults come to Christ. In the first years, he tried and worked and prayed, but no one wanted to start a church with him. No one would come to worship. He felt defeated and didn't know what to do.

Then he noticed that many of the youth and children would come to see him. They had a lot of needs. Alphonso began to serve them, providing food and school uniforms. Eventually, with God's help, he built a school. That led to starting a medical clinic and then a hospital. Finally, he built a sanctuary for worship.

In 2010, everything changed when a massive earthquake rocked Haiti, killing 200,000 people. Thankfully, the earthquake hit during recess at Alphonso's school. All the children were outside playing soccer. But every one of his buildings collapsed. Had the children been inside, they would have been severely injured or killed.

Alphonso was distraught when he saw the damage. He told the Lord, "God, it took thirty-four years to build these buildings, but it only took thirty-four seconds to bring them all down. I'm done."

Alphonso made plans to leave with his wife and move to Florida, where they would live with his extended family.

But as they were preparing to leave, a child came to him and asked, "Pastor Alphonso, who will care for us if you leave?" As he told my friend Wesley, Alphonso believed that was a message from God and decided to stay. He rebuilt the school and a little sanctuary. He brought in children who were left fatherless and motherless.

Can you imagine the crisis of faith that might come if everything you had worked for was torn down in a minute?

GOD IS GREAT, GOD IS GOOD

As kids, we probably all grew up hearing the prayer, "God is great, God is good. Let us thank Him for our food." That brief prayer conveys that God is both great—full of power and majesty—and good, doing good for people.

Some churches start their worship service by saying, "God is good." The people shout back, "All the time." The worship leader then asks, "And all the time?" The church responds, "God is good."

But is that really true? Is God good all the time? What about when an earthquake comes? Is God good then? What about when someone has to suffer abuse, not once but over and over? What about when a pandemic covers the planet? What about when someone hears a cancer diagnosis? What about when a business fails that was thought to be a God-given dream?

The Bible makes the bold claim that God is good *all* the time. Psalm 23:6 (ESV) says, *"Surely goodness and mercy shall follow me* **all** *the days of my life."*

The Bible does not say, "Surely goodness and mercy will be showered on me *some* days," or "Surely goodness and love will be granted to me on *most* days." No, it confidently proclaims, *"Surely goodness and mercy shall follow me all the days of my life."*

> **KING DAVID WAS ALWAYS AWARE OF GOD'S GOODNESS AND LOVE, EVEN WHEN HE FELT THE THREAT OF DEATH, FACED ENEMIES, OR LACKED FOOD AND SAFETY.**

The shepherd-king David wrote this psalm. Every time he turned around, God's goodness was there. When David walked through the valley, felt the threat of death, faced enemies, or lacked food and safety, God's love was there for him. It's as if God's love was pursuing him. He didn't have to beg God for it. He didn't have to prove his worth to receive God's love. God's goodness just followed him.

Through Jeremiah, God says, "I have good plans for you. I have a future that I want you to enjoy. My plans aren't going to bring evil to your life, but good." (See Jeremiah 29:11.)

When we experience difficult circumstances, we may struggle to believe in God's consistent goodness. Life can knock the breath out of us.

A PICTURE OF HEAVEN

I once saw on social media a touching video of a wedding in which the groom surprised his bride by having her students serve as attendants. The video showed the smiling children coming down the aisle in beautiful dresses and little tuxedos. Every one of them had Down's syndrome. The bride and groom were smiling and crying. All the wedding guests were smiling and crying. *I* was smiling and crying! It was a picture of heaven.

We know that children with Down's syndrome are full of blessings and so much love, but when they are born, parents feel the weight of raising a child with so many struggles. They might find themselves asking, "God, why is this happening?"

I know many women who have experienced infertility or miscarriages. Some have lost children after fifteen or even twenty weeks of pregnancy. In those circumstances, it's not hard to wonder, "God, are You good?"

Circumstances make us question God's goodness.

George Müller trusted in God for everything, but he wasn't shielded from trouble. He suffered as he sought to care for children while completely depending on the Lord. In fact, he almost reached a breaking point on December 18, 1841. Here's what he said in his autobiographical narrative:

> There is now the greatest need, and only fourpence in hand...yet I fully believe the Lord will supply us this day also with all that is required....The Lord was saying by this poverty, "I will now see whether you truly lean upon me, and whether you truly look to me." Of all the seasons that I had ever passed through since I had been living in this way, up to that time, I never knew any period in which my faith was tried so sharply as during the four months from December 12, 1841 to April 12, 1842.[35]

On February 25, 1842, he wrote:

> Greater than now our need had never been. Our trials of faith have never been so sharp as during this week. Indeed, so much so, that most of the laborers felt to-day considerably tried. Yet neither this day has the Lord suffered us to be confounded. Through a remarkable circumstance one of the laborers obtained some money this morning, so that all the need of to-day could be amply met.[36]

35. Müller, *The Life of Trust.*
36. Ibid.

Time and time again, Müller discovered that God was faithful. God provided when the need seemed unbearable, whether the need was money, food, supplies, or clothing. Müller trusted in God's Word that proclaimed God is good *all* the time.

> For **the LORD is good** and *his love endures forever; his faithfulness continues through all generations.* (Psalm 100:5)

> *The* LORD, *the* LORD *God, merciful and gracious, longsuffering, and* **abounding in goodness** *and truth.* (Exodus 34:6 NKJV)

> *The* LORD *is* **good to all***; he has compassion on all he has made.* (Psalm 145:9)

> *The* LORD *is* **good***, a stronghold in the day of trouble; he knows those who take refuge in him.* (Nahum 1:7 ESV)

The greatest way that God reveals His goodness is by giving us His Son, Jesus Christ. Jesus laid down His life for us. In Romans 5:6 (NLT), Paul says, *"When we were utterly helpless, Christ came at just the right time and died for us sinners."*

JESUS DIED FOR US WHEN WE WEREN'T EVEN REMOTELY GOOD, WHEN WE DIDN'T DESERVE ANYTHING FROM GOD EXCEPT PUNISHMENT.

In other words, Jesus died for us when we weren't even remotely good. We didn't deserve anything from God's hand except punishment. According to Paul's letter to the early church at Philippi, none of our good deeds, acts of kindness, or giving to others can earn us God's love. They are like garbage or filthy rags compared to the gift of Jesus Christ. (See Philippians 3:8; compare Isaiah 64:6.)

God's good gifts to us have nothing to do with our worth or merit. They depend entirely on God's worth and merit.

Do you struggle to believe that God is good? Do you believe that God is good to you in spite of your faults and failures?

You may not know what the future holds, but God knows the plans He has for you. They are good plans. They are the best plans you could have. No matter how bad your circumstances are, you can trust that your life is going somewhere good when you trust in God.

Believe God is good.

Confess God's goodness in prayer.

Ask in faith for what you need.

PRAYER PRINCIPLE #11:

God's goodness will follow you all the days of your life.

12

UP IN THE CLOUDS

One thing I ask from the LORD, this only do I seek: that I may dwell in the house of the LORD all the days of my life, to gaze on the beauty of the LORD and to seek him in his temple.
—Psalm 27:4

One of my favorite Disney movies is *UP*. It's the story of a seventy-eight-year-old retired balloon salesman named Carl. When Carl was a kid, he dreamed of going to South America to a place called Paradise Falls. A neighborhood friend, Ellie, also wanted to go there. She dreamed of moving the abandoned house that was their "clubhouse" to Paradise Falls.

Carl and Ellie grew up together, fell in love, got married, and bought the abandoned house. They frequently said that they would one day go to South America. Then life became hard. Ellie suffered a miscarriage and was told she couldn't have a biological child. Devastated, they made plans to move to Paradise Falls. They saved money, but something always came up to prevent them from taking the trip. Finally, an elderly Carl arranged for the journey, but Ellie became ill and died.

The story picks up with Carl in that same house. A lot has changed, however. Skyscrapers surround his tiny house. Carl feels pressure to sell, but he won't budge. He's bitter. He's kind of a curmudgeon. He's stuck. He is living a one-dimensional kind of life. He walks to the mailbox every day in a straight line and walks back.

On the way to his mailbox one day, he accidentally injures a construction worker. A judge orders Carl to sell his house and go into a retirement home.

Rather than doing that, Carl hatches a plan. He blows up thousands of helium balloons, secures them to the house, and then launches up into the air to go to South America.

There's a whole lot more to the story, but by the end of the movie, he's had an incredible adventure. The house indeed makes it to Paradise Falls, but Carl returns to the old neighborhood and starts living again. There's something cathartic about going up into the clouds.

A METAPHOR FOR LIFE ASCENT

Carl unburdens himself. He lets go of everything holding him back. *UP* is a kind of metaphor for his life ascent. What happens up in the clouds transforms his life back on earth.

Lots of people are one-dimensional. They get up, go to work, come home, walk the dog, eat dinner, watch television, go to bed…and then do the same things all over again the next day. They're not growing. Maybe they're in a rut because life became too painful. Maybe some dreams led to disappointment. For some, such a life is just fine. But for others, it's just one dull line in a boring, never-ending movie—like *Groundhog Day*, but without the wit, charm, and spiritual growth.

MANY CHRISTIANS ARE LIVING IN A TWO-DIMENSIONAL WORLD. THEY HAVE NO IDEA HOW MUCH MORE THERE IS TO THE LIFE OF GOD.

Then there are two-dimensional people. They can move not only from north to south but also east to west. They think that life is great and they have it all figured out because they can move in these different directions. They have goals. They're accomplished. They have a good reputation. But all that they have is a horizontal outlook, never knowing how much they are missing in another dimension.

Lots of Christians live in this zone. They do the church things and busy religious activities. They know the God-talk. They talk about the body of Christ, missions, evangelism, and spiritual gifts. But they're still living in a two-dimensional world. They have no idea how much more there is to the life of God. They talk about being free, but you get the sense they're really not free. They have heard the psalmist say, *"Taste and see that the LORD is good"* (Psalm 34:8), but they have never tasted. Deep down, they believe that there are celestial realms to be explored, that communion with the living God is really possible, and that they were created to be not just living creatures, but alive in a world of grace and wonder.

THE JOY OF PURSUING GOD

Three-dimensional Christians are different. They have learned to go *up*. Worship is no longer horizontal, but vertical. Daily life starts to ascend. *Up* is enlarging and releasing and purifying. *Up* is beyond the dust and the traffic and the email; it is vast and beautiful and limitless. *Up* has thrones and rainbows and the sound of trumpets. *Up* is the big picture. *Up* points you to the mountaintop and calls you to climb it. *Up* gives meaning to your horizontal existence.

If you want that kind of life, you must learn to go *up*.

Up is not just belief *in* God, but also the pursuit *of* God. A.W. Tozer said, "To have found God and still to pursue Him is the soul's paradox of love."

David had encountered the living God as a little boy; but still he wrote:

One thing I ask from the LORD, this only do I seek: that I may dwell in the house of the LORD all the days of my life, to gaze on the beauty of the LORD and to seek him in his temple. (Psalm 27:4)

Having learned about a life that was always going up before God, David wanted more every day. He wasn't satisfied with walking back and forth to the temple once a week or even once a day. He wanted to dwell in the house of the Lord. He wanted to see the beauty for himself.

George Müller knew such a life. His journal is full of stories of intimacy with God. Such closeness led Müller to say that he had received fifty thousand answers to prayer.

Early in his ministry, Müller became ill and needed to leave Bristol to recuperate. Some friends persuaded him to stay at their home on the Isle of Wight. One evening, after spending time with his hosts, Müller retired to his room. He wanted to sleep, but he also desired to pray beforehand.

Müller recounted what happened after praying a short time:

> The coldness of the night was a temptation to me to pray no further. However, the Lord did help me fall upon my knees; and no sooner had I commenced praying than he shone into my soul, and gave me such a spirit of prayer as I had not enjoyed for many weeks. He graciously once more revived his work in my heart. I enjoyed that nearness to God and fervency in prayer, for more than an hour, for which my soul had been panting for many weeks past...I went to bed especially happy, and awoke this morning in great peace.[37]

That's what can happen when Christians learn to go up. They find themselves happy in the Lord. That is a state of the soul no circumstance can touch, however painful or draining.

Sometimes going up requires first going down, bowing low in humility. It may start with weariness and confession, expressing complete dependence on the living God. Yet soon, God will lift you up. James 4:10 says, *"Humble yourselves before the Lord, and he will lift you up."*

Are you humble before God, who transcends all dimensions, inhabiting heaven and earth?

Worship on earth reminds us of the One who sits on the throne. We remember that God alone is worthy and completely holy. God is the Creator; we are the created. God is infinite; we are finite. We are broken

---

37. Müller, *The Life of Trust*.

and sinful and needing grace, but God is full of grace and truth. God is higher, greater, and purer than our minds can comprehend.

Here's how Matt Redman, a worship leader and singer-songwriter, describes the "otherness" of God:

> Otherness gives us a sense that God is so pure, matchless and unique that no one else and nothing else comes even close. He is altogether glorious—unequalled in splendor and unrivalled in power. He is beyond the grasp of human reason—far above the reach of even the loftiest scientific mind. He is inexhaustible, immeasurable and unfathomable—eternal, immortal and invisible. The highest mountain peaks and the deepest canyon depths are just tiny echoes of His proclaimed greatness. And the blazing stars above [are] the faintest emblems of the full measure of His glory.[38]

This is why it says in Hebrews that we are to *"offer to God acceptable worship, with reverence and awe, for our God is a consuming fire"* (Hebrews 12:28–29 ESV). In Psalm 96:9, we're encouraged to *"worship the LORD in the splendor of holiness, tremble before him, all the earth."*

David wanted a greater and greater experience of God. Can you say that the one thing you want, the one thing you seek, is to be in the presence of the living God?

Take some time today to go up to your heavenly Father. Let your soul relax in God's presence. Seek the Lord and ask God to expand your horizons.

Go up.

PRAYER PRINCIPLE #12:

Humble yourself before the Lord, and He will lift you up.

---

38. Matt Redman, "The Otherness of God," *Christianity Today*, accessed August 22, 2021, www.christianitytoday.com/ct/2004/septemberweb-only/theothernessofgod.html.

13

THE BATTLE OF THE THREE ARMIES

We have no power to face this vast army that is attacking us. We do not know what to do, but our eyes are on you.
—2 Chronicles 20:12

My friend Steve was a force of nature. With a larger-than-life personality, Steve loved to laugh and do things for others. He took worn-out wood from fallen trees and construction projects and crafted them into beautiful cutting boards and furniture.

Steve had a lot of pain from past experiences. His life was complicated. I met him when he and some other friends from a local recovery program started attending our church in Dallas. He struggled with addiction for more than forty years and burned out nearly all of his relationships. I think our church was the first group to stick with him when he started to show signs of anger, judgment, and abrasiveness. People around him tended to feel like they were falling into an abyss. His emotional needs were never satisfied.

Jesus made a difference to Steve. For the first time in his life, Steve started to understand grace. His change was powerful. Through Steve's witness, many people were welcomed into church and heard the gospel. Lots of men and women were baptized. Steve felt that God had finally stabilized his life and that he was doing what he was made to do: be a blessing to others and encourage people in their struggles. He began to save for the future and felt like God would soon help him overcome both addiction and poverty.

Unfortunately, Steve's drug abuse had worn down his body over time. He had heart problems and other issues. One day, he started to cough up blood. He was diagnosed with lung cancer, somewhere between stages three and four. He was in a battle. Steve's pain threatened to spiral him back toward addiction.

For Steve, this was a triple threat: addiction, cancer, and limited funds to fight the disease.

A group of us rallied around him. We gave his pain medication to him one or two pills at a time—his decision because he was determined not to relapse. Through the battle, Steve was constantly seeking the Lord. He would often say, "I have to fight this battle my way." For Steve, that meant trusting God to guide him.

I was with him the last week of his life as the cancer overcame his body. To the very end, Steve never became addicted again. In the last days, he didn't need pain medication. The illness caused him to reach out to mend relationships and express his love. I remember the last time I saw him. I dropped him off at the hospital but wasn't allowed to go inside due to the 2020 pandemic. But I believe that when Steve took his last breath, he wasn't alone. Jesus was there to see him over the threshold and welcome him to a new home.

Some may say, "What happened to Steve was a tragedy," but that's simply not true. His life ended in victory. Just like the apostle Paul, Steve could say, *"I have fought the good fight, I have finished the race, I have kept the faith*" (2 Timothy 4:7). When he didn't know what to do, he kept his eyes on God.

TROUBLES WILL COME

In 2 Chronicles 20:1, three armies—the Moabites, Ammonites, and some Meunites— conspired in one massive assault against Judah and their king, Jehoshaphat. The odds weren't in Jehoshaphat's favor.

Honestly, sometimes our odds aren't good either. When trouble comes, it often arrives not with one problem, but two or three of them. Relationship trouble at home can threaten to undermine one's work. Stress at work can lead to depression. Poverty leads to a host of crises, such as not having money for medicine or a clinic visit, which causes emotional stress.

George Müller was a passionate prophet against poverty and despair. He advocated for orphans when they faced a lack of emotional support, wrenching poverty, and disease. Müller took them all in—more than ten thousand children who had nowhere else to turn.

He even took a kind of vow of poverty to identify with Jesus as well as the poor. Early in his ministry, Müller rejected a salary from the first church he pastored because they paid their clergy by renting out pews in the front to the wealthy, while the poor were told to sit in the back.[39] He pointed to the lesson of James 2:2–4:

> *Suppose a man comes into your meeting wearing a gold ring and fine clothes, and a poor man in filthy old clothes also comes in. If you show special attention to the man wearing fine clothes and say, "Here's a good seat for you," but say to the poor man, "You stand there" or "Sit on the floor by my feet," have you not discriminated among yourselves and become judges with evil thoughts?*

Müller took his place with the poor. He trusted God through every circumstance. Sometimes he faced the triple threat of intense poverty, physical ailments, and spiritual distress. In those times, he continued to look to the living God.

---

39. Müller, *The Life of Trust.*

WHEN GEORGE MÜLLER FACED THE TRIPLE THREAT OF INTENSE POVERTY, PHYSICAL AILMENTS, AND SPIRITUAL DISTRESS, HE CONTINUED TO LOOK TO THE LIVING GOD.

When Jehoshaphat faced three armies, he responded as an uncommon leader.

First, he called on the people to seek God: "*Alarmed, Jehoshaphat resolved to inquire of the* LORD, *and he proclaimed a fast for all Judah. The people of Judah came together to seek help from the* LORD; *indeed, they came from every town in Judah to seek him*" (2 Chronicles 20:3–4). They all came together to fast, pray, and seek the Lord.

They said, "God, You gave us this land. You drove out all the inhabitants. We built a temple to worship You and when that temple was dedicated, You promised that if war or deadly plagues or any crisis came, all we needed to do was humble ourselves, pray, and seek Your face, and turn from our wicked ways. Then You would hear from heaven and forgive our sins and heal our land. That's why we're here. We are humbly coming before You because now, God, three armies are advancing on us." (See 2 Chronicles 20:6–9.)

"OUR EYES ARE ON YOU"

Then they prayed one of the most powerful prayers in the Bible:

We have no power to face this vast army that is attacking us. We do not know what to do, but our eyes are on you. (2 Chronicles 20:12)

If you can pray like Jehoshaphat did—declaring, "Lord, we don't know what to do, but our eyes are on You"—then you can know that ultimately, everything will be okay. That's not false hope or pie-in-the-sky thinking. That's trusting in the all-seeing God to see you through.

If you don't know what to do, seek God like Jehoshaphat did. It's so simple, but somehow the hardest thing to do.

Second, Jehoshaphat followed God's Word. He set out to accomplish God's plan for victory. The Spirit of the Lord delivered this message:

You will not have to fight this battle. Take up your positions; stand firm and see the deliverance the LORD *will give you, Judah and Jerusalem. Do not be afraid; do not be discouraged. Go out to face them tomorrow, and the* LORD *will be with you.*   (2 Chronicles 20:17)

When he heard God's voice, Jehoshaphat took action. Notice the active verbs in the Lord's message: Take your position. Stand firm. See the deliverance God will give to you. Go out. Face them.

When God tells you what to do, take action as soon as possible. Jehoshaphat set out, stood, and spoke. When you hear God's voice, you have to be ready to move because the moment can pass quickly. You can't hesitate.

This is where so many people get stuck. They wonder, *Did I really hear the Lord? Is that what You're saying, God? Lord, give me just one more sign to help me know I'm hearing You right.*

A PRO TIP OF FAITH

A friend once shared with me what I have come to call a *pro tip of faith.* He said, "Brent, God can handle your mistakes. God can handle your bumbling through life and His will. What God cannot handle is your lack of action. You must step out even if the first step isn't perfect. You can't wait until you know everything or until God shows you everything to act. Yes, you might make a mistake. You might fail. You might even sin. But Jesus can handle all of that. He can forgive it all. But with the person who hesitates, who buries the talent in the ground, God can't do anything."

> GOD CAN HANDLE YOUR MISTAKES. GOD CAN HANDLE YOUR BUMBLING THROUGH LIFE AND HIS WILL. BUT HE CAN'T DO ANYTHING WHEN YOU HESITATE AND FAIL TO ACT.

Set out in faith believing that God is with you. Stand up on the Rock of Ages. Speak with authority because God will not fail. When God tells you what to do, take action immediately.

Third, before heading into battle, Jehoshaphat praised God:

Jehoshaphat appointed men to sing to the LORD and to praise him for the splendor of his holiness as they went out at the head of the army, saying, "Give thanks to the LORD, for his love endures forever." As they began to sing and praise, the LORD set ambushes against the men of Ammon and Moab and Mount Seir...and they were defeated.
(2 Chronicles 20:21–22)

Who sings as they go into battle? God's people do. Who else in the world but the church comes together and sings? We sing in our homes. We sing when we're together. We sing when we're sad and when we're happy. We keep singing in the middle of the battle. We will keep singing because God is God and God is with us.

Whatever your battle, keep singing. Keep praying. Keep saying, "God, I don't know what to do, but my eyes are on You."

Watch and see how God delivers.

PRAYER PRINCIPLE #13:

When you don't know what to do, keep your eyes on God.

SECTION THREE

FORSAKE SIN

14

THE PRISON OF THE HEART

*And whenever you stand praying, forgive, if you have anything
against anyone, so that your Father also who is in heaven may forgive you your trespasses.*
—Mark 11:25 (ESV)

Could a lack of forgiveness for someone be a reason that you don't experience more answers to prayer?

When I was in my twenties, I carried a lot of anger toward my dad. My perception was that he wasn't present for me emotionally during my growing-up years. That was probably true. There are many other ways, however, to be present for a person. Dad was a good provider, showed up at ball games, and taught me how to play golf. Looking back, I am grateful for the things he did well.

Maybe now that I am a dad who has raised kids and launched them out into the world, I can appreciate just how ridiculously hard it is for a father to be everything that a modern kid needs.

For a season, I felt like my anger toward my dad was a real block in my life. It also seemed to hinder my spiritual life. I frequently felt sad and negative. This is the great irony of clinging to past resentments and bitterness. I once heard that resentment is like drinking poison and then hoping it will kill the person who wronged you. That was true for me. I held my dad as a prisoner within my heart.

UNFORGIVENESS HURTS YOUR HEART

No heart is meant to be a prison.

Over time, I understood that my problem wasn't my dad, but me and my lack of forgiveness. I realized around age thirty that I really hadn't forgiven my father. Failing to forgive, I only hurt myself. Unforgiveness is at the heart of many issues that require counseling. As I worked through my issues in counseling and journaling, I realized that my dad wasn't raised to talk about his problems or feelings. Or maybe he was afraid to do so. He had his own issues related to his own father. It's scary to start down a road that could lead to some real messiness. I also came to realize that he was unequipped to fix what he didn't understand. He had not been given the emotional tools to navigate pain, vulnerability, and healing conversation. It wasn't his fault that he couldn't give what he didn't have.

In the end, there could be no peace without forgiveness. There would be no apology or moment of truth. There would be no breakthrough between him and me. All that was left in my mind was the residue, which was my responsibility.

At a particularly low point in my life, a friend invited me to officiate at his beach wedding at Gulf Shores, Alabama. My family and I were staying a few miles from the beach in a cramped hotel room. For some reason, my heart was particularly burdened with the memory of my dad during that weekend. Maybe it was because we frequently went to the beach when I was a child. Those trips were some of my best memories with my father, but he still seemed far away emotionally.

Feeling that I needed God's peace to help me overcome my unforgiving heart, I got up in the middle of the night and went into the little bathroom. Although I tried to pray, all I could think about was how much I resented my dad. After an hour struggling, I finally felt God's love fill me and I came face to face with my own lack of love. God gave me the strength to utter the words, "I forgive you." Immediately, I felt a weight lift from my shoulders. I knew something in me had changed. I left all my bitterness and resentment toward my dad in that hotel bathroom.

Deep down, I knew that without forgiving him, I would never have real peace and wouldn't be forgiven.

Jesus linked forgiveness with prayer: *"When you stand praying, if you hold anything against anyone, forgive them"* (Mark 11:25). In His model prayer, He also taught that we should pray, *"Forgive us our sins, for we also forgive everyone who sins against us"* (Luke 11:4).

Jesus taught us the importance of forgiving others as we stand before God in prayer because failure to forgive blocks our connection with our heavenly Father. It limits intimacy with God. Failing to forgive signals that one is not approaching God with a posture that all of life is grace.

FORGIVENESS BREAKS THE POWER OF RESENTMENT, RETALIATION, AND BITTERNESS THAT CAN SO EASILY DOMINATE OUR HEARTS.

On the other hand, forgiveness breaks the power of resentment, retaliation, and bitterness that can so easily dominate our hearts. Therefore, Jesus taught, *"If you are offering your gift at the altar and there remember that your brother or sister has something against you, leave your gift there in front of the altar. First go and be reconciled to them; then come and offer your gift"* (Matthew 5:23–24).

We must extend grace to receive grace. We must forgive to be forgiven.

The good news is that God's grace is extended to all.

George Müller once said in a sermon, "There is even the possibility that the greatest thief, the greatest robber, the vilest person that ever lived under heaven, can obtain forgiveness for his crimes. There is grace found in God, since 'He is the God of all Grace,' that whatever amount of grace is needed, it is to be had in Him. It is to be found in God. The greatest sins can be forgiven."[40]

Compared to my sins, my father's sins seem small. If God can forgive me of all of my sins, then surely I can forgive my father and anyone else who harms, offends, or betrays me. My reconciliation to God means that all my relationships can be reconciled.

Müller once noted:

> When thus he is reconciled to God, by faith in the Lord Jesus, and has obtained the forgiveness of his sins, *he has boldness to enter into the presence of God, to make known his requests unto Him*; and the more he is enabled to realize that his sins are forgiven, and that God, for Christ's sake, is well pleased with those who believe on Him, the more ready he will be to come with all his wants, both temporal and spiritual, to his Heavenly Father, that He may supply them.[41]

If we expect to receive anything in prayer, we must first forgive others. When we forgive, we make room in our hearts to receive more answers to prayer.

GOD IS DEEPER STILL

Corrie ten Boom and her family helped many Jews escape from the Nazis during the Holocaust in World War II by hiding them in her home. She believed she was doing the will of God. When the family was arrested, Corrie and her sister Betsie were sent to the Ravensbrück concentration camp. It's hard to imagine the atrocities the two sisters endured. Even so, they held on to faith. Betsie once encouraged Corrie with the words, "There is no pit so deep that He [God] is not deeper still."

Twelve days later, Corrie was suddenly released due to a clerical error. One week later, all of the women in her age group, including Betsie, were sent to the gas chambers.

---

40. From a sermon preached at Bethesda Chapel, Great George Street, Bristol, on Sunday evening, March 28, 1897. Archived at www.georgemuller.org/devotional/the-god-of-all-grace-make-you-perfect-stablish-you, accessed August 21, 2021.
41. Mueller, *Answers to Prayer*, 80.

Corrie became a writer and speaker. Her message was that God forgives even the worst of sins. In 1947, Corrie spoke at a church in Munich, Germany. She preached to the congregation, "When we confess our sins, God casts them into the deepest ocean, gone forever."

As people stood up to leave, she saw a balding, heavyset man in a gray overcoat. And she remembered him, a former Ravensbrück guard who had forced women prisoners to strip and walk past him naked.

He approached her and thrust his hand out in greeting. "A fine message, fräulein! How good it is to know that, as you say, all our sins are at the bottom of the sea." He didn't remember that she had been there. But she remembered him. She froze and fumbled for her pocketbook rather than take his hand.

"You mentioned Ravensbrück in your talk," he continued. "I was a guard there. But since that time, I have become a Christian. I know that God has forgiven me for the cruel things I did there, but I would like to hear it from your lips as well." He put his hand out and said, "Fräulein, will you forgive me?"

FORGIVENESS IS AN ACT OF WILL

Corrie knew she had to do it. God's message is clear. If we do not forgive, how can our Father in heaven forgive us?

She stood there with coldness clutching her heart. Forgiveness is not an emotion, she knew. It is an act of the will. So, she prayed silently, "Jesus, help me! I can lift my hand. I can do that much. You supply the feeling." Mechanically, she thrust her hand into the one stretched out to her. As she did, an incredible sensation took place. A current started in her shoulder, raced down her arm, and sprang into their joined hands.

Then a healing warmth flooded her whole being, and she said, "I forgive you, brother! With all my heart!"[42]

Do you want more power in prayer?

---

42. Corrie Ten Boom, a story from *The Hiding Place*, "Guideposts Classics: Corrie ten Boom on Forgiveness," accessed August 21, 2021, www.guideposts.org/better-living/positive-living/guideposts-classics-corrie-ten-boom-forgiveness.

Do you want to find release from a burden you have carried for too long?

Whom do you need to forgive?

Remember how much you have been forgiven. Lift your hand and ask God to supply the feeling. God can help you. You have been forgiven much, so you can forgive.

With all your heart.

PRAYER PRINCIPLE #14:

Failing to forgive blocks power in prayer.

15

CUT IT OUT

If your right eye causes you to stumble, gouge it out and throw it away. It is better for you to lose one part of your body than for your whole body to be thrown into hell.
—Matthew 5:29

In 1921, Dr. Evan O'Neill Kane was the chief surgeon at Kane Summit Hospital in Kane, Pennsylvania. After thirty-seven years of practicing medicine, Kane had performed more than four thousand appendectomies. Contrary to standard medical practice at the time, he believed that using general anesthesia for all surgeries wasn't the best option, that a local anesthetic would be better in many cases. But who could test his theory?

Finally, the perfect case presented itself. Kane injected novocaine at the site, made the incision, clamped the blood vessels, and set about locating the appendix. Then with his brother, also a surgeon, and other medical professionals standing by, Kane removed the inflamed organ.

His own.[43]

In the Sermon on the Mount, Jesus describes a very personal and precise surgery to deal with sin. This procedure is to be used with the largest and the smallest of sins.

Jesus doesn't say, "It would be good for you to deal with that at some point." He doesn't say, "You know, it's not so bad. Everybody has a vice or two." No, He states in very simple terms without any confusion: you need to cut out the sin immediately.

Why would Jesus advocate for such a drastic measure? Because your soul is at stake. Persistent sin ultimately will lead you down a destructive road. In the same way a bad appendix poisons the body, unaddressed sin poisons the soul.

IN THE SAME WAY A BAD APPENDIX POISONS THE BODY, UNADDRESSED SIN POISONS THE SOUL.

Of course, Jesus is speaking in hyperbole. He would never ask you to actually gouge out your eye as a solution to the temptations and sins of lust or coveting. But He is challenging you to not give sin any room in the house of your heart.

THE HIGH COST OF SIN

Sin blocks your relationship with God and paralyzes prayer. George Müller said, "It is not possible to live in sin, and at the same time, by communion with God, draw down from heaven everything one needs for this life."[44]

43. C. J. Clancy, "Dr. Evan O'Neill Kane: Irish American surgeon famous for self-surgery," *IrishCentral*, www.irishcentral.com/opinion/others/dr-evan-o-neill-kane-self-surgery.
44. Müller, *The Life of Trust*.

We usually think that sin is a negative reality that divides us and separates us from God. But sin also impacts the positive gifts God wants to give us.

Mike Yaconelli, one of the twentieth century's great leaders in practical ministry, said:

> Sin is more than turning our backs on God, it is turning our backs on life! Immorality is much more than adultery and dishonesty, it is living drab, colorless, dreary, stale, unimaginative lives. The greatest enemy of Christianity may be people who say they believe in Jesus but who are no longer astonished and amazed. Jesus Christ came to rescue us from listlessness as well as lostness; He came to save us from flat souls as well as corrupted souls.[45]

Rather than asking, "What does God not want me to do?" we need to ask ourselves, "What am I not receiving because I am allowing sin to linger in my life? What prayers are going unanswered? What joy have I lost because I chose other things?"

Sin costs you more than it's worth.

We might think of someone like George Müller as a kind of super-saint. However, Müller had no such opinion of himself. He once mused in his diary on questions that many people had likely asked him: "How would it be if the funds for the orphans were reduced to nothing, and those who were in the work had nothing of their own to give? Suppose a mealtime arrived, and you had no food for the children?"

Müller wrote:

> Thus indeed it could happen, for our hearts are *"desperately wicked"* (Jeremiah 17:9). If we should ever be left to ourselves by either no longer depending on the living God or by allowing sin a place in our hearts (Psalm 66:18), then such a state of things, we have reason to believe, would occur. But as long as we are enabled to trust in the living God, and as long as, though falling short in

---

45. Michael Yaconelli, *Dangerous Wonder: The Adventure of Childlike Faith* (Colorado Springs, CO: NavPress, 2003).

every way of what we might be and ought to be, we are at least kept from living in sin, such a state of things cannot occur.[46]

I believe Müller was right. Rather than presuming on God, Müller was just stating a spiritual reality. Those who deal with sin seriously and quickly can expect that God will be happy with such a life. All of us stumble and fall. However, we can expect that God will continue to provide all that we need when we are sustained by God's grace to keep trusting in Him. In other words, when we actively deal with sin, we can expect that God's blessings will be more fully opened to us.

> **WHEN WE ACTIVELY DEAL WITH SIN, WE CAN EXPECT THAT GOD'S BLESSINGS WILL BE MORE FULLY OPENED TO US.**

What sin needs to be excised from your life?

Lust?

Greed?

A pattern of cheating?

Judgmental thinking?

Name that sin and deal with it now before your heavenly Father. Ask for forgiveness. Pray for help in battling that sin in the future. If you fail again, trust in God's mercy. Jesus said we need to ask for forgiveness whenever we pray as He taught us to pray. (See Matthew 6:12.)

There's nothing we can do to make eternal atonement for our sins. Only through the cross of Christ have our sins been separated from us as far as the east is from the west. (See Psalm 103:12.) Thanks be to God that He *"does not treat us as our sins deserve or repay us according to our iniquities"* (Psalm 103:10). God doesn't overlook our sin or dismiss it as unimportant. In God's view, sin is so serious that it had to be dealt with at great cost to Himself.

---

46. Müller, *Release the Power of Prayer*, 31.

Jesus died for you. You can stop carrying around your sins because He died for you. You can stop trying to be perfect because He died for you. You can forgive other people as you have been forgiven because He died for you. You can learn to be patient and kind because He died for you.

Not only that, but because He rose again from the grave, you can now experience victory over sin. The same power that raised Jesus from the grave now helps you to have power over sin and death.

> *The Spirit of God, who raised Jesus from the dead, lives in you. And just as God raised Christ Jesus from the dead, he will give life to your mortal bodies by this same Spirit living within you.*
> (Romans 8:11 NLT)

As you confess sin and repeatedly seek forgiveness, over time, God will give you victory. Your most tempting sin will become your testimony.

But you cannot use Christ's gift of forgiveness as an excuse for continued sin. Jesus's teaching still stands: cut it out. Yes, you need God's help, but don't expect God to do for you what Christ has commanded you to do. God's grace is free, but each follower of Jesus is called to take up the cross, forsake sin, and depend on God alone as Jesus did. (See Matthew 16:24; Proverbs 28:13; and 1 John 2:6, respectively.)

CHASING AFTER FAKE REWARDS

Legendary preacher, theology professor, and storyteller Fred Craddock gave a sermon about meeting a retired talking greyhound. The sleek animal lay at his feet while he asked about its racing days.

"So why did you retire from racing?" Fred asked.

"I didn't retire. Is that what they told you?"

"Well, did you get injured?"

"No, that's not what happened," said the dog.

"Did you stop winning?"

"No," said the dog. "I spent ten years as a professional, racing greyhound. That means ten years of running around that track day after day, seven days a week, with other dogs, chasing that rabbit. Well, one day, I got up close and got a good look at that rabbit. And do you know what? It was a fake! I spent my whole life chasing a fake rabbit! I didn't retire; I quit!"[47]

Like the greyhound's fake rabbit, sin tricks us into chasing after it, promising happiness and delivering anything but.

Time to quit that sin. It's worthless.

PRAYER PRINCIPLE #15:

Persistent sin prevents the flow of God's gifts.

---

47. Fred Craddock (1928–2015) was known for his humorous, folksy preaching style, and there are many variations of this story online. For more from Craddock, see his book *Craddock Stories* (St. Louis, MO: Chalice Press, 2001).

16

DIDN'T SEE IT COMING

Be sober-minded; be watchful. Your adversary the devil prowls around like a roaring lion, seeking someone to devour.
—1 Peter 5:8 (ESV)

One of my favorite running routes in Dallas took me past the zoo. I loved how I could be in the heart of the city but still see elephants, zebras, and giraffes from a bridge overlooking a wide savannah.

The view made me think back to times in Africa when I observed such animals from the safety of a vehicle while on a safari. There was a terrifying episode in which our vehicle was just feet away from a roaring lion. On another occasion, we were rushed by an elephant.

One day, I ran past the zoo and paused to watch a massive elephant lumbering in the grass. Then I ran around the bend and into the adjacent neighborhood. This route had some sidewalks, but often I was just on the shoulder of the road, having to watch for debris. Normally this path was very safe. On that day, however, I failed to see a small, sharp piece of metal fence jutting up from the grass. The invisible spike was connected to a larger section of fence where the grass was overgrown.

The top of my right foot caught on the metal piece. The fence was so heavy and I was moving so fast that I crashed to the ground face-first. It all happened in a micro-second.

Fortunately, my elbows extended to break some of my fall. My forehead, however, still slammed into the ground. The breath was immediately knocked from my lungs. I stayed motionless for about a minute, doing a personal inventory as I checked my arms, legs, head, and shoulders. I was wondering, *Am I okay? Is anything broken?* I was bruised in several places, but thank God, that was the extent of my injuries.

I surveyed my surroundings. And just six inches from where my forehead hit the ground, a large shard of broken glass stuck up in the dirt. Had I landed only a half-foot away, I could have lost an eye or suffered a brain injury.

Some might say that the greatest threat to my life was the fierce animals—elephants, lions, or wildebeests—just beyond the road.

Not so.

THE DANGER OF "LITTLE" SINS

The greatest danger was so small that I didn't even see it coming.

That's true of the temptations and sins in our lives. We are often in more danger due to a minor transgression than a huge moral failure. The small threat seems so harmless that it's overlooked until it turns into something more. There is no follower of Jesus Christ who won't face threats like these.

> WE ARE OFTEN IN MORE DANGER DUE TO A MINOR TRANSGRESSION THAN A HUGE MORAL FAILURE. SMALL THREATS SEEM SO HARMLESS BUT CAN GROW INTO SOMETHING MORE.

Someone who is unfaithful in their marriage may be caught in a great public scandal. Infidelity, however, doesn't happen in one major moment of failure. It starts with a thought that is allowed to ferment, leading to an indiscretion that may be a little larger—a flirtation at the office, a suggestive text message—which leads to a big fall.

The little things matter. This is why Paul wrote to the Corinthians, *"So, if you think you are standing firm, be careful that you don't fall!"* (1 Corinthians 10:12).

Peter taught the church to always be sober-minded and watchful because the devil is like a roaring lion, watching to see who can be devoured. *Sober* suggests someone who is mentally attentive and self-controlled. *Watchful* means awake and alert. Even though God is all-powerful and provides help for His children in temptation, we cannot afford to relax our guard spiritually. It is vital that we recognize that Satan is relentless and waits in the shadows for an opportunity to feed.

Jesus Himself was stalked by Satan in the wilderness. He was tempted to turn stones into bread—a simple, subtle temptation—but Jesus knew that a quick fix to His hunger would actually be a denial of His simple reliance on God. (See Matthew 4:1–11.)

He didn't give into the temptation. As His followers, however, we give in again and again. Jesus taught that if we ever find ourselves tripped up and giving in to sin, the right response is not to abide it, ignore it, or rationalize it. Instead, the Lord tells us to acknowledge it, ask for forgiveness, and cut it out immediately.

If your hand or your foot causes you to stumble, cut it off and throw it away. It is better for you to enter life maimed or crippled than to have two hands or two feet and be thrown into eternal fire. And if your eye causes you to stumble, gouge it out and throw it away. It is better for you to enter life with one eye than to have two eyes and be thrown into the fire of hell. (Matthew 18:8–9)

As mentioned previously, Jesus doesn't literally want us to gouge out an eye or cut off a foot. His vivid language suggests, however, that sin is serious and must be dealt with quickly. There are eternal consequences to our earthly choices.

There are also real-time consequences, such as in the area of answered prayer.

> **WE CAN'T BE LIFTED INTO GOD'S PRESENCE OR EXPECT OUR PRAYERS TO BE ANSWERED IF SOME KNOWN SIN IS ALLOWED TO REMAIN.**

We can't be lifted into God's presence if some known sin is allowed to remain. In such a state, we should expect none of our prayers to be answered.

George Müller once said, "We must have 'white robes,' else we cannot enter into the presence of God. Our own sins, which are compared to filthy garments, must be removed, and we must solely and simply trust in the merits and sufferings of the Lord Jesus Christ, and thus, by the power of his atonement, be made clean from all our sins."[48]

Müller knew that God had cleansed him. He also knew how little sins could turn into bigger problems.

MÜLLER STRUGGLED WITH SIN

In his autobiography, Müller wrote, "My father, who educated his children on worldly principles, gave us much money, considering our age. The result was, that it led me and my brother into many sins. Before I was ten years old, I repeatedly took of the government money which was intrusted to my father...till one day...he detected my theft, by depositing a counted sum in the room where I was, and leaving me to myself for a while. Being thus left alone, I took some of the money and hid it under my foot in my shoe."[49]

His father caught him, but punishments failed to stop Müller. Instead his tactics became more furtive.

---

48. George Muller, "White Robes," accessed August 21, 2021, www.georgemuller.org/quotes/white-robes.
49. Müller, *The Life of Trust*.

Müller's sinful habits eventually landed him in jail after he stayed at two expensive hotels with no money to pay the bills. He related, "I now found myself, at the age of sixteen, an inmate of the same dwelling with thieves and murderers. I was locked up in this place day and night, without permission to leave my cell."[50] He spent Christmas there. For twenty-four days—from December 18, 1821, to January 12, 1822—he was confined to the prison. His father obtained his release by paying the inn debt and his maintenance at the jail; he also furnished enough money for his son to return home.

Müller had finally discovered the consequences of sin, but it still took some time before he sought the Lord.

His path didn't begin with a huge heist. It was the product of dozens and dozens of indiscretions, petty thefts, and deceit. The grace of God redeemed the time and used it to bring Müller closer to Him.

NON-PRAYER TIME AFFECTS PRAYER

One of the greatest lessons I have learned about the life of prayer is that *what I do when I'm not praying impacts the power of my prayers.* An evening of filling my mind with impure thoughts leads to a scattered prayer time in the morning. A poor series of choices, such as not getting enough rest or pursuing mindless activities, affects my fruitfulness during the week. Negative thoughts crowd thoughts full of praise. Failing to forgive blocks my access to God's grace to receive forgiveness.

When I fail to address sin, I deny the total dependence I have on God for everything. My prayers lack power. My life feels drained. In those moments, it takes much effort and prayer, but I ask God for mercy and assistance to help me get back into a state of being sober-minded and alert. I pray that God would renew my discipline. I ask for protection from future attacks.

What about you?

Is there something you keep getting snagged on, something that could ultimately cause a great fall? Is there something hidden that needs to come into the light?

50. Ibid.

ASK GOD TO HELP YOU NAME YOUR SIN, FACE IT, AND CUT IT OUT. YOU CAN'T SAVE YOURSELF. YOU NEED THE HELP OF HEAVEN.

Ask God to help you name it, face it, and cut it out. You can't save yourself. You need the help of heaven.

Today, make a list of anything that could be causing you to lack power in prayer. Then make a plan to remove those obstacles one by one from your life.

Pray that God would strengthen you as you make a change.

Watch how God uses that good choice to help you run faster and farther in the pursuit of His kingdom.

PRAYER PRINCIPLE #16:

Little snags lessen prayer power.

17

A TOWERING SHIP
IN THE SAND

If any of you lacks wisdom, you should ask God, who gives gener-
ously to all without finding fault, and it will be given to you.
—James 1:5

Newcastle, Australia, is an industrial port city about seventy-five miles north of Sydney. On the morning of June 8, 2007, about fifty ships were waiting in Newcastle's harbor to load coal.

Then a storm rolled in, battering the ships and coast for thirty-six hours. The port authority radioed to warn the waiting ships to "move out to sea," but ten of them ignored the warning.

As the storm worsened, the Panamanian carrier *Pasha Bulker* was swept toward the coast. The ship's captain was reportedly having break-fast below deck while his less-experienced crew was trying to weather the storm. When he finally took command of the ship, it was out of control—and he made a fatal error that caused the huge vessel to surf to the beach.[51]

---

51. "Captain at breakfast as ship sailed to doom," *The Sydney Morning Herald*, www. smh.com.au/national/captain-at-breakfast-as-ship-sailed-to-doom-20071013-gdrbzq.html.

At 10 a.m., the *Pasha Bulker* ran aground at Nobbys Beach right by the city center. Although it hadn't picked up its cargo yet, the massive vessel still weighed more than forty tons.

Both the crew and city leaders were afraid it would impact the city. So they loaded the ship with ballast to sink it deeper into the sand and prevent it from moving farther up the beach.

It sat there for a month.

The owner scrambled to figure out how to get the ship to sea again. One jokester briefly advertised the ship for sale on eBay; bids climbed to $16 million before the auction was shut down.

In the meantime, the *Pasha Bulker* became a tourist attraction. Crowds gathered to stare at the ship. Ice cream trucks and coffee stands popped up. As one visitor noted, "Thousands of people were drawn to the sight of a towering ship resting quietly in the sand...It was a spontaneous and quite delightful display of community."[52]

WHO IS YOUR SOUL'S CAPTAIN?

What can be learned from this cautionary tale? Here are two questions to guide you toward a personal application.

First, who is the captain of your soul?

I was once asked to perform a funeral for a kind but generally self-centered man. Right before I stood up to speak, the program called for a slideshow set to the music of Frank Sinatra's "My Way." The man lived a comfortable life. He made and spent a lot of money. Unfortunately, when it came to summing up his life, I did not know how much of a difference he had made in the lives of others.

You could say that his ship never left the harbor of his own comfort. He never risked the adventure of a life with a mission. He was in charge of his own life. It wasn't a bad life, but it just didn't seem to be the best life.

Who is in charge of *your* life?

52. Mike Frost, "The Alphabet of Grace: B is for Breathtaking," blog post September 12, 2020, accessed August 21, 2021, mikefrost.net/the-alphabet-of-grace-b-is-for-breathtaking.

Second, where do you get wisdom?

The *Pasha Bulker* was designed for a purpose: to carry cargo. The captain's decisions and actions, however, caused that mission to run aground. The captain valued his own wisdom too much and the wisdom of others too little.

> **GEORGE MÜLLER LAUNCHED ORPHANAGES TO STRENGTHEN PEOPLE'S FAITH. CARING FOR HUNGRY, HOMELESS CHILDREN WAS A SECONDARY PURPOSE.**

You might think that George Müller launched orphanages for the sole purpose of caring for hungry, homeless children, but that was a secondary purpose. His first purpose was to strengthen the faith of the people of Bristol, England, and beyond.

Müller frequently met men and women who worked fourteen or sixteen hours a day, causing their bodies to suffer, their souls to become lean, and their hearts to have no enjoyment in God. He sensed that people worked only to make an income, with little trust in God to provide for them. He longed to see them "have their faith strengthened."[53] There was no taking hold of the truth that we must first seek God's kingdom and righteousness, *"and all these things will be given to you as well"* (Matthew 6:33).

PROOF OF GOD'S FAITHFULNESS

Müller wanted people to ultimately know it was not their work that supported their families, but the work of the living God, who would feed and clothe them, by His means in His timing, when they were unable to work.

Müller opened the orphanages with the intent of creating a kind of "visible proof that our God and Father is the same faithful God that he

---

53. Müller, *The Life of Trust.*

ever was—as willing as ever to prove himself the living God, in our day as formerly, to all who put their trust in him."[54]

He wanted men and women to know the wisdom that God can give for any situation. He wanted people to trust God even when life felt like a shipwreck. He wanted them to take God at His word and rely on it.

Such wisdom requires faith. James wrote:

If any of you lacks wisdom, you should ask God, who gives generously to all without finding fault, and it will be given to you. (James 1:5)

That includes all of us. We all need heaven's help in navigating life's storms. When you need wisdom, all you need to do is ask God for it. God grants wisdom generously *"without finding fault."* In other words, it doesn't matter how far away you have strayed. It doesn't matter how badly you have made a mess of things. It doesn't matter if you have relied on your own wisdom a hundred times before turning to God. God gives wisdom generously—lavishly, freely, and abundantly—without holding your past against you.

WE ALL NEED HEAVEN'S HELP IN NAVIGATING LIFE'S STORMS. WHEN YOU NEED WISDOM, ALL YOU NEED TO DO IS ASK GOD FOR IT.

If you have sinned or stubbornly shaken a fist at God, don't let your past define your future. God can forgive your worst attitudes and actions. Ask God in confidence for what you need, believing that God's character and promises trump any past offenses.

But when you ask, you must believe and not doubt, because the one who doubts is like a wave of the sea, blown and tossed by the wind.
(James 1:6)

Some other Bible translations say you must ask *"in faith."* Believing and having faith means trusting in God and having confidence in Him. It's

---

54. Ibid.

going before God with the quiet confidence that God is there, that God hears, and that God answers.

God answers only one kind of prayer: the prayer of faith. When healing two blind men who told Jesus they believed He could make them see, the Lord said, *"According to your faith let it be done to you"* (Matthew 9:29).

What is faith? You may say, "I believe God *can* do it." But that's not faith. Of course God can do it, whether you believe it or don't believe it. You may also say, "I believe God *might* do it." That's not faith either. That's hoping for a good outcome.

But if you say, "I believe God *will* do it," that is faith.

When you trust in God with all of your life, live according to God's will, forgive others like Jesus taught, give your life away like Jesus gave His life away, make God your delight, and ask in faith, you can expect that God will answer your prayer.

That's what it means to make God your captain.

God gives wisdom generously. However, *"the one who doubts…should not expect to receive anything from the Lord"* (James 1:6–7).

People who doubt are on their own. They're kind of half-in, half-out, looking to God but mostly depending on their own wisdom. Their life is not done God's way, but "my way." They may be fine for a while, but it's likely that they will soon run aground, never embracing the purpose for which God created them.

> **THOSE WHO DEPEND ON THEIR OWN WISDOM MAY BE FINE FOR A WHILE, BUT IT'S LIKELY THAT THEY WILL SOON RUN AGROUND.**

Like the *Pasha Bulker*, the towering ship that became a sideshow, their lives end up being little more than an interesting slideshow set to a Sinatra tune.

Jesus told His disciples to take up the cross. The cross represents purpose. Jesus's cross was His mission, dying for the sins of all humanity. Your cross will also be painful and costly at times as you lay down your life for the sake of others.

MADE FOR A MISSION

You were made for a mission. Like the *Pasha Bulker*, you weren't made for the harbor. You were made to deliver the precious cargo of God's love, hope, and peace into the shipwrecked lives of others.

You were made for more.

One thing is certain: you and I will never become what God made us to be if we declare ourselves to be captains. There is only *"one Lord, one faith, one baptism; one God and Father of all, who is over all and through all and in all"* (Ephesians 4:5–6).

Do you lack wisdom? Ask God today. God gives generously without finding fault. Ask and it will be given to you.

Do you need purpose? God can reveal that to you, too.

Let today be guided by the living God. Pray now for God's wisdom. Listen for God's communications. Don't ignore the warnings. Take off the captain's hat and take up the cross.

PRAYER PRINCIPLE #17:

A life apart from God's wisdom eventually runs aground.

18

START OVER

Draw near to God, and he will draw near to you.
—James 4:8 (ESV)

In 1998, Ralph and Sandra Fisher of LaGrange, Texas, lost their beloved pet, Chance. According to Ralph, Chance was a "big bundle of just loving." He licked their faces and nuzzled up to them. This was unusual behavior for a full-grown Brahman bull weighing two thousand pounds.

The kids loved him. Chance was more like a dog than a bull. He followed the family around the yard. They took him to conventions and barbecues. He made appearances in movies and on television shows.

When Chance died at age nineteen, the family was devastated.

But Ralph had heard about a new Texas A&M University animal-cloning program and decided to apply. And about eleven months later, the first cloned bull was born.

Can you guess what they named him?

Second Chance.

Bizarrely, when Ralph brought him home, Second Chance went straight to the spot where Chance used to lie in the yard. He walked like

Chance walked. He made the same sounds and had the same mannerisms as Chance. Ralph believed he had his beloved Chance back, although the doctor warned him several times that it was not the same animal.

Everything seemed to be fine until Second Chance's fourth birthday party. The bull slammed Ralph to the ground, horns digging in. Ralph said later, "He might just have to go through a little stage and settle down."

When you love, you see what you want to see.

Nearly two years later, Second Chance suddenly gored Ralph in the crotch, requiring eighty stitches. The attack also caused a hairline fracture on Ralph's spine and broke his nose.

Even so, Ralph was not ready to give up on Second Chance. "I'm just thinking that, you know, we just have to have a lot of faith in things to work out. So I forgive him, you know? I just shouldn't have been that close," he said.[55]

How far does love go?

GOD SEES THE BEST IN US. WHEN WE WOUND GOD, GOD LOVES US ANYWAY. GOD FORGIVES AND KEEPS ON FORGIVING.

Ralph's love for Second Chance reflects how God extravagantly loves us. God sees the best in us. When we wound God, God loves us anyway. God forgives and keeps on forgiving. Why? Because when you love, you see what you want to see.

CONVICTED BUT UNCHANGED

God saw the best in George Müller. He received multiple chances to return to the Lord when his life was off track. In school, Müller was often stirred when the Scriptures were read in chapel. But he continued to fall

---

55. This story was told on the podcast *This American Life*, Episode 291, "Reunited (and It Feels So Good)," accessed August 21, 2021, www.thisamericanlife.org/291/reunited-and-it-feels-so-good/act-two-6.

away—convicted but unchanged, desiring God's will but desiring his own will more.

Rather than reading the Bible, he spent his time reading spiritual tracts, missionary papers, sermons, and biographies of godly persons. It was a form of spirituality, but Müller was always circling the periphery. He wrote:

> I never had been at any time of my life in the habit of reading the Holy Scriptures. When under fifteen years of age, I occasionally read a little of them at school; afterwards God's precious book was entirely laid aside, so that I never read one single chapter of it till it pleased God to begin a work of grace in my heart…I practically preferred, for the first four years of my divine life, the works of uninspired men to the oracles of the living God.[56]

While these books and tracts were good, they gave Müller little power for living out the Christian life. As such, Müller often drifted away from God, weak and without the power of the Holy Spirit. Then he had what he called his "second conversion." He wrote:

> The Lord enabled me to put it to the test of experience, by laying aside commentaries, and almost every other book, and simply reading the Word of God and studying it. The result of this was, that the first evening that I shut myself into my room, to give myself to prayer and meditation over the Scriptures, I learned more in a few hours than I had done during a period of several months previously. *But the particular difference was, that I received real strength for my soul in doing so.*[57]

Müller's soul was quickened. He was full of energy and joy. It was a new start and the blessed beginning of a life of trust in the living God.

---

56. Müller, *The Life of Trust*.
57. Ibid.

GOD LOVES TO REDEEM

God wouldn't give up on Müller just as Ralph wouldn't give up on Second Chance.

God won't give up on you either.

It doesn't matter if you have neglected God. The important thing is what you do going forward. If you draw near to God, God will draw near to you. God won't hold your past sins against you. God won't stomp on your shame. *"A broken and contrite heart, O God, you will not despise"* (Psalm 51:17 ESV).

God is a God of second, third, and fourth chances. God loves to redeem.

IF YOU ARE IN NEED OF A SECOND CHANCE, YOU MUST FIRST RECOGNIZE THAT YOUR WAY ISN'T WORKING, AND YOU NEED TO SEEK GOD WITH ALL YOUR HEART.

If you find yourself in need of a second chance, how do you return to God?

The first step is to realize that you are tired of the way you're living now. In Alcoholics Anonymous culture, there's a saying: "I'm sick and tired of being sick and tired." It's time for you to say, "I'm fed up. I'm tired of spiritual weakness. I'm tired of feeling overworked, unfruitful, and distant from my heavenly Father."

God says, *"You will seek me and find me when you seek me with all your heart"* (Jeremiah 29:13).

The second step is to admit your sins. Name your failures. Ask the Spirit to help you confess your sins as well as reveal the root cause of those sins. *"If we confess our sins, he is faithful and just and will forgive us our sins and purify us from all unrighteousness"* (1 John 1:9).

The last step in returning to God is to let go of your life. Give God control of your heart and see what He can do with it.

The word *forgiveness* in the Bible suggests a hurling away of something from something else. It's a separation and total detachment. When God forgives you, God lets it go.

Every day, you can pray, "God, I'm letting go of my life today. I'm placing it in Your hands. Thank You for forgiving me and giving me another chance to turn to You today."

Ralph's love for Second Chance is almost comical.

Such is the love of God towards us.

Every prayer is a kind of second chance. It's an opportunity to believe. Turning toward God can open fresh possibilities for you.

GIVING A SECOND CHANCE

In November 2004 on Long Island, New York, a group of teenagers went on a joyride using a stolen credit card. They used it to rent DVDs and video games; they purchased cookies, drinks, shrimp, Christmas hats, and a frozen turkey. One of them decided to throw the turkey out the window of their car.

The twenty-pound bird crashed through the windshield of a car driven by Victoria Ruvolo. The impact broke every bone in her face, damaged her left eye socket, and bruised her brain. She required extensive reconstructive surgery to her face and months of rehabilitation before she could return to work nine months later.

Suffolk County prosecutors had wanted the turkey tosser, Ryan Cushing, then eighteen, to serve the maximum of twenty-five years in prison for first-degree assault and other offenses. But Victoria argued that a long sentence would only turn him into a hardened criminal.

Because she asked for amnesty, Ryan received a six-month prison sentence with five years' probation of community service and psychiatric help.

At his sentencing, he walked over to where Victoria was sitting. As she later recalled:

All he was doing was crying, crying profusely. He looked at me and said, "I never meant this to happen to you, I prayed for you every day. I'm so glad you're doing well." Then this motherly instinct just came over me and all I could do was take him and cuddle him like a child and tell him, "Just do something good with your life, take this experience and do something good with your life."[58]

Some people could not understand how Victoria could be so forgiving, but as she explained, "God had given me a second chance and I wanted to pass it on."[59]

In light of God's amazing love and forgiveness, you can start again, too. You can live again. Ask God for a fresh start. Ask God for a new heart. God won't despise your broken heart. God will help you start again. You won't be disappointed.

PRAYER PRINCIPLE #18:

Every prayer is another chance to trust God more.

58. Victoria Ruvolo, The Forgiveness Project, www.theforgivenessproject.com/stories-library/victoria-ruvolo.
59. Ibid.

19

GUARD YOUR CASTLE

Finally, brothers and sisters, whatever is true, whatever is noble,
whatever is right, whatever is pure, whatever is lovely, whatever
is admirable—if anything is excellent or praiseworthy—
think about such things.
—Philippians 4:8

There's an old tale about a magnificent castle in Ireland that was left uninhabited and thus had fallen into decay. From time to time, nearby peasants would take stones from the castle for their construction needs, whether they wanted to build a pigsty or repair a road.

The owner, Lord Londonderry, was visiting his estate and decided to put an end to this vandalism. He ordered a six-foot-high wall to keep out trespassers. Then he went away.

When he returned three or four years later, to his amazement, the castle was gone. In its place was a large stone wall enclosing...nothing. He sent for the agent in charge and demanded to know, "Where is the castle?"

The agent replied, "The castle is it? Bedad, I built the wall with it, my lord. Is it for me to be going miles for materials with the finest stones in Ireland beside me?"[60]

All believers face challenges, attacks, temptations, hard circumstances, and setbacks. What we prize the most can be seriously threatened by outside forces. But the greatest battle every believer faces is the battle within.

It's the battle of the mind.

As a person thinks in their heart, so they are. (See Proverbs 23:7.) Our thoughts form the foundation for our lives, revealed in our actions and words. Our thoughts determine our destiny. Because this is true, our minds are always under siege by the enemy.

YOUR MIND IS A CASTLE THAT MUST BE GUARDED. STONE BY STONE, IT CAN BE CARRIED AWAY OR MADE INTO SOMETHING OTHER THAN WHAT GOD HAS PLANNED.

Your mind is a castle that has to be guarded. Decay is always possible. Stone by stone, it can be carried away or made into something other than what God has planned.

GUARDING YOUR THOUGHTS

No one ever sets out to become a negative or pessimistic person. But the enemy's number-one target is your thoughts. If the enemy can control your thoughts, then he can control your attitudes, self-image, and actions. Those actions will lead to bad habits, inappropriate patterns of thinking, and negative responses. Over time, those habits form your character, which in turn informs your destiny.

---

60. Fred T. Hodgson, "Myths, Superstitions, Romance and Humor of Architecture," *Architecture and Building*, September 11, 1897, 97.

This is why Scripture says, "*Set your minds on things above, not on things that are on the earth*" (Colossians 3:2 ESV). You have to stay focused on the higher things of God. Otherwise, you should expect nothing in prayer.

Paul writes, "*Rejoice in the Lord always. I will say it again: Rejoice!*" (Philippians 4:4). He goes on to outline a way to keep your mind focused on positive things. But let's be clear: Paul is not teaching the *power of positive thinking*. His answer is not, "Just keep a positive frame of mind." His answer is, "Rejoice!" Paul is counseling believers to fix their minds not on general, positive thoughts but on the character of God and His goodness.

The Greek word for *rejoice* here can also be translated "farewell." Paul is making his final farewell to the Philippian church. He is essentially saying, "Don't be a victim to all of your problems. Don't get overwhelmed by the trouble inside of you, within the church, or through outside circumstances. Don't let your problems take your joy away." Paul then says, "*Let your reasonableness be known to everyone. The Lord is at hand*" (Philippians 4:5 ESV). Along with joy, reasonableness and gentleness are critical to your witness in the world.

Paul reminds the Philippians that God is very near. God hasn't abandoned you. However, Paul also means, "The time of God is near. The time is coming when everything will be put right, and all of the suffering and despair of this world will be over."

Because God is near and the time is at hand, you must keep praying. Keep thanking God and asking for what you need. Jesus taught that His followers should always pray and never give up.

When all understanding fails, then the peace of God will set a guard around your heart and mind in Christ Jesus. (See Philippians 4:7.) The word *guard* is a military term. Like a sentry on duty, God's peace will guard your heart and mind. God will protect you from temptation and from falling into sin when you feel lost and confused.

If you feel threatened, pushed around by your circumstances, or opposed at every turn, know that you don't have to lose your soul. In full confidence, you can forbear with others and experience joy in your heart, devoting time to prayer, thanksgiving, and praise. If God's peace is within you, you don't have to keep scanning the horizon for threats. You don't have to worry about bad news coming through a phone call, email, or social media.

> **IF GOD'S PEACE IS WITHIN YOU, YOU DON'T HAVE TO KEEP SCANNING THE HORIZON FOR THREATS.**

THE BEST THINGS TO PONDER

Paul gives this advice:

Finally, brothers and sisters, whatever is true, whatever is noble, whatever is right, whatever is pure, whatever is lovely, whatever is admirable—if anything is excellent or praiseworthy—think about such things. (Philippians 4:8)

"*Whatever is true…*" Specifically, Paul is talking about the truth of the gospel as the standard for your life. Titus 1:2 speaks of "*the hope of eternal life, which God, who does not lie, promised before the beginning of time.*" To focus on true things also means to reflect on what you know is right and sound in the world, not based on deception or half-truths.

"*Whatever is noble…*" The word *noble* means "worthy of reverence," "dignified," or "elevated." It's noble when a teenager finds a wallet full of money in the school hallway, then takes it to the lost-and-found rather than keeping it. It's noble when someone gives up their seat on the bus for an elderly person. We are to think on such things.

"*Whatever is right…*" This can also mean whatever is righteous, honorable, or virtuous. Think on things that are just and fair. These are things that aren't tainted or shady. This part of the Scripture compels us to focus on God's standard of righteousness in harmony with God's will for us.

"*Whatever is pure…*" The word *pure* means "free from defilement, stainless, spotless." It has to do with the state of our minds and the acts of our bodies. We are called to be pure in a very messy world. Paul writes, "*Do you not know that your body is a temple of the Holy Spirit within you, whom you have from God? You are not your own, for you were bought with a price. So glorify God in your body"* (1 Corinthians 6:19–20 ESV).

"Whatever is lovely…" This passage references conduct that is pleasing, beautiful to behold. God wants us to be people of beauty, creating beautiful things that nurture a sense of awe in us. In the same way, God desires that we push away anything that is crass or debased.

"Whatever is admirable…" *Admirable* could also be translated "worthy of a good report," referring to things worth telling someone else about. Thinking on *admirable* things means not focusing on or reporting the faults and sins of others. It means reflecting on the best in each person. Think about those things that are excellent and worthy of praise.

You can decide what you think. Every day, you can choose your attitude. You can choose the content that enters your mind. Make a decision to set your mind on things above.

PRAYING FOR GOD'S PEACE

Have confidence in the sentry God has placed over your life. God's peace can protect your mind and heart. All you need to do is let it. Every day you can pray, "God, watch over my life. Protect me and deliver me from evil. Things are going to happen today that may shake my confidence in You and dampen my spirit. I don't want my mind taken away stone by stone."

George Müller kept his eyes on the Lord through good times and bad. In seeking God's direction for his ministry future, he often waited days, weeks, or months in prayerful discernment. In December 1850, while praying about whether to expand his efforts to help more orphans, he wrote:

I have the fullest and most peaceful assurance that he will clearly show me his will…This calmness of mind, this having no will of my own in the matter, this only wishing to please my heavenly Father in it, this only seeking his and not my honor in it; this state of heart, I say, is the fullest assurance to me that my heart is not under a fleshly excitement, and that if I am helped thus to go on I shall know the will of God to the full.[61]

Müller's mind was calm, stayed on God.

Could you have a similar state of mind such that you would feel continual peace and joy in God's presence as you reflect on His goodness and faithfulness? Could you also *"think about such things"*?

"You will keep in perfect peace those whose minds are steadfast, because they trust in you" (Isaiah 26:3).

Why not fix your eyes on God right now and receive His peace?

PRAYER PRINCIPLE #19:

A steadfast mind leads to perfect peace.s

---

61. Müller, *The Life of Trust.*

SECTION FOUR

EXERCISE FAITH

20

BUILT TO LAST

*Let patience have its perfect work, that you may be perfect and
complete, lacking nothing.*
—James 1:4 (NKJV)

At one time, all the great cathedrals in Europe were built with stone.
That's why they're still around. They were built by master stonemasons and
skilled artisans. In medieval times, it took seven years to become a master
stonemason. Today, it still takes three or four years of classroom instruction and on-the-job training. Someone who wants to be a master must first
be an apprentice, learning to read blueprints, mix mortar, determine the
best stones for specific positions, and how to use various tools, such as a
level, a square, and a trowel. It takes a lot of time and patience to become
a master.

Some people don't have that kind of time and patience. Sadly, many
people aren't interested in that kind of quality.

So a little over a hundred years ago, builders began putting a one-inch
veneer of stone on building exteriors instead of actual stones. What's seen
on a building may be just a thin layer of rock. It could even be cement that

is colored and shaped to look like stone. The average person can't tell the difference.

This technique, called stone cladding, costs about a third of real stone. It's not load bearing and won't last as long as real stone. And it doesn't require a stonemason to install it.

A person can have the veneer of a Christian life without really having the built-to-last change of heart and lifestyle underneath. Most people throw up a veneer of prayer rather than investing in a life of powerful, durable prayer. A veneer of prayer will quickly crumble. It won't endure.

> **MOST PEOPLE THROW UP A VENEER OF PRAYER RATHER THAN INVESTING IN A LIFE OF POWERFUL, DURABLE PRAYER THAT PERSISTS FOR A LIFETIME.**

Do you just apply a thin layer of prayer to a flimsy structure dedicated to yourself? Or are you someone who knows how to build a strong intimacy with God through prayer that persists for a lifetime?

WAITING ON GOD IN PRAYER

On November 4, 1845, after much prayer and counsel with fellow believers, George Müller became convinced that God wanted him to move out of the rental properties on Wilson Street in Bristol, England. He believed that God was calling him to build a larger, more suitable home for children on the outskirts of town. He began to pray every day for financial means and direction concerning which property God had chosen for the new work. The project would cost at least ten thousand pounds.[62]

Thirty-five days after Müller was convinced of God's will to build the new orphan house, not a single penny had been given to the work. "Nevertheless," Müller wrote, "this did not in the least discourage me, but my assurance that God, in his own time and his own way, would give the

---

62. Müller, *The Life of Trust*.

means, increased more and more."[63] His diary outlines his daily waiting upon the Lord in patience and faith.

December 24: "No further donation yet. But my hope in God is unshaken. He most assuredly will help." January 6: "I am now quietly waiting the Lord's pleasure." January 31: "It is now eighty-nine days since I have been daily waiting upon God about the building of the Orphan House. The time seems to me now near when the Lord will give us a piece of ground, and I told the brethren and sisters so this evening, after our usual Saturday evening prayer meeting."[64]

February 2: "Today I heard of suitable and cheap land on Ashley Down." February 3: "Saw the land. It is the most desirable of all I have seen." February 4: "This evening I called on the owner of the land on Ashley Down...but he was not at home. As I, however, had been informed that I should find him at his house of business, I went there, but did not find him there either, as he had just before left. I might have called again at his residence...but I did not do so, judging that there was the hand of God in my not finding him at either place; and I judged it best therefore not to force the matter, but to 'let patience have her perfect work.'"[65]

Müller saw the owner the next day and learned that he had awakened at three that morning and couldn't go back to sleep until five. Lying awake, the owner couldn't get the piece of land off his mind and the possibility of selling it to build the orphan house. He decided that if Müller did indeed want the land, he would sell it to him for 120 pounds per acre instead of his asking price of 200 pounds.

On February 5, 1846, Müller wrote:

Observe the hand of God in my not finding the owner at home last evening! The Lord meant to speak to his servant first about this matter, during a sleepless night, and to lead him fully to decide before I had seen him.[66]

Müller obviously had a deep and abiding faith. Even when things didn't go his way, he kept believing. Even when it seemed like God wasn't

63. Ibid.
64. Ibid.
65. Ibid.
66. Ibid.

moving, Müller kept his eyes heavenward and watched for God's handiwork. He knew that God would be the one who ultimately built the house, or it wouldn't be built at all.

George Müller was a master mason of prayer.

How about you? Is that the kind of person of prayer you are? Is this the kind of disciple you want to be? If so, know that it will mean great change for you. The gospel is about deep change.

> *As you come to him, the living Stone—rejected by humans but chosen by God and precious to him—you also, like living stones, are being built into a spiritual house to be a holy priesthood, offering spiritual sacrifices acceptable to God through Jesus Christ. (1 Peter 2:4–5)*

God did not make you to be what somebody else wants you to be. God did not make you to be what your parents want you to be, what your girlfriend or boyfriend wants you to be, what your spouse wants you to be, or what your boss or your friends want you to be.

God made you to be you—a stone with a very special place in God's house.

You are formed into that strong structure by praying, investing in meditating on God's Word, imitating the life of Jesus, and persevering by faith.

Always remember that you aren't the cornerstone. Christ is. You and other believers are *"built on the foundation of the apostles and prophets, with Christ Jesus himself as the chief cornerstone. In him the whole building is joined together and rises to become a holy temple in the Lord"* (Ephesians 2:20–21).

Today you can say, "From this day on, I will not let others press me into their mold. I wasn't made to be part of someone else's blueprint. I'm going to be what God wants me to be. I'm going to do what God wants me to do. Everything will rest on Him."

Remember, He's the stone the builders rejected. (See Psalm 118:22; Matthew 21:42.) If you start to trust in Him on a deeper level and depend on Him through patient prayer like never before, people might start to reject you, too. They may think you're crazy. You may be ostracized or ridiculed by your family, your coworkers, or friends. But you will never be rejected by God. Being a part of God's spiritual house is the most secure place you can be.

> **IF YOU START TO DEPEND ON GOD THROUGH PATIENT PRAYER LIKE NEVER BEFORE, PEOPLE MIGHT START TO REJECT YOU, BUT YOU WILL NEVER BE REJECTED BY GOD.**

When I was in Israel a few years ago, there was a young man joining our pilgrimage who asked a lot of questions. I could tell that he was really soaking up the experience. He knew the Bible stories, but he confessed that he really didn't know God deeply. The Holy Land was awakening his desire for a deeper faith and a surer foundation.

NOT ENOUGH...BUT JUST RIGHT

On one of our long van rides, he told me that he often felt like he wasn't "enough." He wasn't a strong enough man or a good enough husband. He wasn't a church member that others could lean on. I just listened. He seemed to be working something out. He knew that he needed the kind of life that lasts. He just didn't know how to have that kind of life.

On one of our last days in Jerusalem, we stood before the great Western Wall, where massive stones had been put together by Herod the Great more than two thousand years ago. We were marveling at these stones, some of them weighing 160,000 pounds, when he said, "I'm like one of these stones."

"What do you mean?" I asked.

"None of them were perfect when they were brought out of the quarry," he said. "Someone took them and shaped them and placed them in just the right spot. I'm realizing that it doesn't matter that I'm not perfect. That stone was enough while it was in the quarry. It just had to be shaped and fitted into the right spot."

God sees you like that. God sees the masterpiece in the mess. But you have to be willing to be fitted and fashioned. You have to be willing to be changed. Not many people like change. Change is hard. A great work of art or a magnificent building doesn't happen overnight. A deeper life of trust, patiently hoping in the Lord, takes time, attention, and work.

Believe that patience will do its work until you are perfect and complete, lacking nothing.

Pray today that God would shape you. Pray that God would strengthen you. Pray that God would secure you on the cornerstone, Jesus Christ.

Don't just talk about prayer. Pray now. Be real before your heavenly Father. Build a solid structure of faithful prayer that will last a lifetime.

PRAYER PRINCIPLE #20:

The lasting life is built on solid, strong prayer.

21

ACRES OF DIAMONDS

*Do not store up for yourselves treasures on earth, where moths and
vermin destroy, and where thieves break in and steal. But store up
for yourselves treasures in heaven, where moths and vermin do not
destroy, and where thieves do not break in and steal. For where
your treasure is, there your heart will be also.*
—Matthew 6:19–21

There was once a Persian farmer named Ali Hafed who lived near the
River Indus. Although he was a wealthy man, when an old Buddhist priest
started talking to him about diamonds, Ali Hafed experienced discontent. He sold his farm, left his family, and traveled throughout the world,
searching for diamonds. After spending all his money, now wretched and
poor, he threw himself into the sea and drowned.

Meanwhile, the man who had purchased Ali Hafed's farm was watering his camel in a garden brook when he noticed a flash of light in the
water. He pulled out a pretty black stone that seemed to have an eye of light
and put it on his mantel. A few days later, the Buddhist priest came for a
visit and spotted the glimmer on the mantel. Excitedly, he told the new

landowner what it was and together they stirred up the sand in the garden brook and uncovered more gems.

Thus began the famous diamond mine of Golconda, India.

This true story was told over 6,000 times by Dr. Russell Conwell, the founder of Temple University. It illustrates the principle that often what is of great value is closer than we think.[67]

GOD DELIGHTS IN GIVING GIFTS

You and I are standing on acres of diamonds. Through prayer, we have enormous resources available to us through the power of the Creator of the universe. We don't have to travel far away to find what we need. God is a loving Father who delights to share with His children the gifts of His kingdom. (See Luke 12:32.)

If Ali Hafed had only known how to study the land, identify the shape and look of uncut diamonds, and search diligently, he would have discovered diamonds under his very feet.

In a similar way, if we could have eyes to see the resources available to us, seek God with the whole of our lives, and ask God when we need something, we would experience what Jesus called *"treasures in heaven."*

MORE IS NEVER ENOUGH

The problem is that our culture is consumed with consumerism. We put our trust in the things of the earth rather than the things that are above. When we gather more and more for ourselves, we discover that more and more is never enough. We hoard what we have, thinking we'll need it for another day. We could be sharing with someone else in need, but fear makes us grip too tightly onto God's good gifts.

---

67. Russell H. Conwell, *Acres of Diamonds*, www.gutenberg.org/files/368/368-h/368-h. htm.

WHEN WE GATHER MORE AND MORE FOR OURSELVES, WE DISCOVER THAT IT'S NEVER ENOUGH, AND WE HOARD WHAT WE HAVE.

Christians in America often look to God for *spiritual* supplies like encouragement, strength, and hope, but not for *temporal* supplies. We read Jesus's words about not storing up wealth on earth and trusting God to ensure that we have enough today. Yet somehow, we just can't imagine giving up control of these things to receive a greater inheritance through the Lord.

George Müller embraced a radical economic model. His life demonstrates an alternative to the way most people approach wealth and possessions.

Early in his ministry, Müller committed to trusting in God for everything, including his temporal supplies, his family, and the orphans under his care. He never asked anyone for money or solicited donations on the children's behalf but instead prayed in faith and watched to see God supply. By the end of his ministry, without asking for a dime, Müller noted, "Not one out of a hundred ministers has such a large salary."[68]

Of course, he gave almost all of it away. His goal each year was to have a little less in savings than the previous year, even if God poured more into his hands year by year.

Some may say that would be a very stressful life. But Müller said his life was a happy one. He encouraged everyone to consider how they make a living through the lens of faith and generosity.

His secret was simple: prayer in simple reliance on the living God. Is it possible for us to live in complete dependence on God?

FOUR KEYS TO A LIFE OF TRUST

Müller offers four keys to living such a life.

First, a person must "not merely say that he trusts in God, but must really do so. Often individuals profess to trust in God, but they embrace

68. Müller, *The Life of Trust*.

every opportunity where they may directly or indirectly be able to expose their need, and thus seek to induce persons to help them. I do not say it is wrong to make known our wants; but I do say it ill agrees with trust in God to expose our wants for the sake of inducing persons to help us."

Second, "the individual who desires to go this way must be willing to be rich or poor, as the Lord pleases. He must be willing to know what it is to have an abundance or scarcely anything. He must be willing to leave this world without any possessions."

Third, that person must "be willing to take the money in God's way, not merely in large sums, but in small. Again and again have I had a single shilling given or sent to me. To have refused such tokens of Christian love would have been ungracious."

Fourth, that person must "be willing to live as the Lord's steward. If any one were to begin this way of living, and did not communicate out of that which the Lord gives to him, but hoard it up, or if he would live up to his income, as it is called, then the Lord, who influences the hearts of his children to help him with means, would soon cause those channels to be dried up."[69]

DIAMONDS FROM MÜLLER'S LIFE

You may think, *How does this apply to me?* You may be on a fixed income in your retirement years. You may receive a salary or paycheck in the way that most Americans do, not through donations, but through your work.

It's true that Müller's life seems extreme and impractical. But I believe that we can glean some "diamonds" of truth from his story, too.

> WE SHOULD NEVER FORGET THE SOURCE OF OUR BLESSINGS. NO MATTER HOW THEY CAME TO US, THEY ARE GIFTS FROM GOD.

---

69. Ibid.

The first truth is that we should never forget the source of our blessings. We should always give thanks for what God gives to us, whether through traditional or unconventional means. Most of us have more than enough. Few of us recognize on a regular basis, much less a daily basis, that God is the source of our daily bread. Trusting in God and God alone is the goal of faith. Giving thanks reaffirms such trust.

The second truth is that we must be ready to live on less if God chooses to use us more for God's glory. That doesn't mean we'll be asked to live on less. It could be that God will increase our supply so that we can be more generous with others. The point is that God is looking for *available* people who will answer the call, even if it's costly.

The third truth is that God indeed has given "acres of diamonds" to us in the form of small and simple gifts. Blessing others doesn't mean spending large sums. God wants to use the little things we have to help others, too. A smile. A small gift. A phone call. A note of encouragement. A helping hand. All of these can be given because God has already richly blessed us.

Jesus says, "*One who is faithful in a very little is also faithful in much, and one who is dishonest in a very little is also dishonest in much*" (Luke 16:10 ESV).

The fourth truth is that we must always think of ourselves as stewards, not owners. If God has trusted us with much, God expects much in the way we steward those resources.

This is what it means to store up treasures in heaven.

A HEART FOR YOUTH

In his book *Messy Spirituality*, Mike Yaconelli tells a story he calls "Gertie: the Old Lady Who Infiltrated a Youth Group" about a seventy-six-year-old woman who became concerned for the youth of her church.

Gertie decided to volunteer to help with the high school group. She took photos of every youth and made cards that listed biographical information. This helped her remember details about each person.

Gertie would stand at the door of the youth room every Sunday evening. As the students came in, she welcomed them by name. When the youth learned that Gertie knew a lot of Scripture, they started coming to her with questions and struggles.

Ten years of youth ministry later, at age eighty-six, Gertie had three strokes. The youth were devastated. They wanted to help her but didn't know what to do.

One afternoon after reading the book *Tuesdays with Morrie*, the youth pastor had an idea.

"Gertie," he said, "I want to do your funeral."

"I know," she said. "I want you to do my funeral. But there's a problem. I'm not dead yet."

"Yes, I know," he said, "but I want to do your funeral while you are alive so that our youth can tell you how much you mean to them and our church."

She loved the idea. They planned the living service. When the evening of the service arrived, the place was packed. Many people who had graduated from college, married, and had their own children came back for the service. Story after story was told about the difference Gertie made to them.

At the end of the service, a group of high school students gathered in the back of the room. They had a special surprise planned.

Gertie loved expensive, designer perfume, especially *Beautiful* by Estée Lauder.

The young people walked down the aisle and huddled together as they were hiding something. When they got to Gertie, they revealed a giant, costly bottle of *Beautiful*. They poured it over her feet in thanks for what she had done.[70]

Before Jesus was crucified, a woman anointed His feet with costly perfume to prepare Him for His burial. (See Mark 14:3–9.) Jesus said of her, *"She did what she could"* (verse 8). Gertie had given what she could, too. It was more than enough to provide a rich blessing for the youth. Gertie's offering of love, time, and thoughtfulness will echo through eternity.

---

70. Mike Yaconelli. *Messy Spirituality*, (Grand Rapids, MI: Zondervan, 2007), 150–151.

YOU MAY THINK YOU DON'T HAVE MUCH TO GIVE, BUT GOD HAS A RICH SUPPLY ALREADY AVAILABLE TO YOU.

You may think you don't have much to give. You may not know the rich supply already available to you.

You may be unaware that you're standing on acres of diamonds. God is able to supply all that you need and more than enough to share with others.

Through prayer, a diamond is within your grasp today.

PRAYER PRINCIPLE #21:

To pick up a treasure, you'll have to kneel.

22

IT'S YOUR TURN

But thanks be to God! He gives us the victory
through our Lord Jesus Christ.
—1 Corinthians 15:57

Shalane Flanagan won the women's division of the New York City Marathon in 2017. Her victory was about more than just a personal athletic achievement. She was the first American woman to win in forty years. She finished the race in a phenomenal 2 hours, 26 minutes, and 53 seconds.

Shalane calls herself "unapologetically competitive" and relentless to win every race that she runs. But perhaps her greater accomplishment is found in the way she nurtures and promotes other runners. That's a rare trait for a professional runner. Usually, running is a cutthroat sport. Runners typically don't help each other.

That's where Shalane is different, however. Every one of her eleven training partners has made it to the Olympics while training with her. She encourages, challenges, and helps other runners.

They call it the Shalane Flanagan Effect. She serves as a kind of rocket booster to help others take off. Shalane has inspired thousands of professional and amateur athletes to train, break personal records, and run with endurance.

After Shalane won the New York City Marathon, fellow U.S. marathoner Desiree Linden shared congratulations on Twitter. Shalane replied, "Now it's your turn."[71] Five months later, Desiree won the Boston Marathon—the first U.S. woman in thirty-three years to win that race.

American Molly Huddle tweeted praise for Desiree's victory, to which the latter replied, "Head up. You're next."[72]

How much do you think about the people who are following after you?

FOLLOWING AFTER JESUS

Millions and millions of Christians around the world celebrate Easter every year. For far too many, however, the story has become boring and routine. People know the basic facts. Jesus was arrested. Despite His innocence, He was crucified like a criminal. Three days later, God raised Him from the dead. Easter Sunday pulls all of these events together, and people get used to the story. We make Easter a one-dimensional holiday rather than allowing it to be to a multi-dimensional, life-transforming way of life.

JESUS'S RESURRECTION DIDN'T JUST PROVE THERE IS LIFE AFTER DEATH. IT PROVES THAT THERE'S LIFE BEYOND YOUR GRAVE.

71. Hayden Bird, "After saying, 'It's your turn,' Shalane Flanagan celebrates Desiree Linden's win," boston.com, April 16, 2018, accessed August 23, 2021, www.boston.com/sports/boston-marathon/2018/04/16/after-saying-its-your-turn-shalane-flanagan-celebrates-desiree-lindens-boston-marathon-win.

72. Nicole Lyn Pesce, "Pro runners Deena Kastor and Molly Huddle tell Moneyish why more American women are winning marathons," November 4, 2018, accessed August 23, 2021, www.marketwatch.com/story/pro-runners-deena-kastor-and-molly-huddle-tell-moneyish-why-more-american-women-are-winning-marathons-2018-11-04.

We miss that the story of the resurrection isn't just Jesus's story—*it's our story as well*. Jesus won the victory, but the victory wasn't just about Him. Jesus's death and resurrection didn't just prove there is life after death. The resurrection proves *you* can have life after death, that there's life beyond *your* grave.

If He has risen from the grave, then you too can rise. Now it's your turn.

You can rise above your fears. You can rise over your temptations. One day, you'll rise to a new life in Him for eternity.

In the resurrection, the powers of death and discouragement were put on notice. That world is coming to an end. A new world is being born. This means that together we can rise as community because Jesus has won the victory. There's power in the death and resurrection of Jesus Christ, and it's not just for the super-saints. He shares it *with you*.

You can learn to pray with more peace and joy in your heavenly Father, just as Jesus prayed.

You can pray for the next generation, knowing that your prayers really do make a difference.

George Müller invested his life in three areas: caring for orphans; distributing Bibles and tracts through the Scriptural Knowledge Institute; and pastoring a local church. He wrote about God's provision and faithfulness in a book he called his *Narrative*. He loved encouraging others through his story and seeing how God blessed others through his experience.

A LESSON THAT GROWS A MINISTRY

In November 1856, a young Irishman named James McQuilkin became a follower of Jesus Christ. When he came across Müller's autobiography, he immediately began to apply the principles of prayer and faith described in the book. He said to himself, "See what Mr. Müller obtains simply by prayer. Thus *I* may obtain blessing by prayer."

McQuilkin prayed that God would give him a spiritual companion to share the gospel. Soon a young man joined him. The two set out to preach and teach others about Christ. Then two more young men joined them after a prayer meeting. The four men began to meet and pray every Friday evening, asking God to bless their ministry efforts. One evening, a farmhand accepted Christ at the end of the worship service. He joined them, as well as another student. By then, their number was six.

By early 1859, they were preaching regularly and sharing their testimony in churches across Ireland. Some people mocked them, but others accepted the message.

When they went to Belfast, Ireland, in May 1859, the Holy Spirit started to move in a mighty way. Tens of thousands of people came to the Lord through this group of young believers. The work spread to Scotland and other countries.

Müller recounts their story in his book and then invites us to see "what delight God has in answering abundantly the believing prayers of His children."[73]

What is the biggest prayer you can pray? Multiply that by one thousand or one million. That's how big God thinks.

IT MAY BE THAT YOUR PRAYERS TODAY WON'T BE ANSWERED FOR A GENERATION OR MORE—BUT THEY WILL EVENTUALLY BEAR FRUIT.

It may be that your prayers today won't be answered for a generation or more. It may be that the seeds you plant now will provide shade for generations to come.

Before we too quickly move to the next generation, what is God calling you to do *now* through faith in the resurrected Christ? What is the biggest dream you can imagine? What is the thing that you *must* do in the power of the Holy Spirit?

It's your turn.

---

73. Müller, *The Life of Trust.*

God wants to share with you Jesus's victory over fear. You don't have to be afraid of illness, suffering, or pain. Nothing can separate you from God's love in Christ Jesus.

God wants to share with you Jesus's victory over sin. Jesus died the death we deserved. He shares the free gift of eternal life. Paul summarized the resurrection message in this way:

> If you declare with your mouth, "Jesus is Lord," and believe in your heart that God raised him from the dead, you will be saved.
>
> (Romans 10:9)

Finally, God wants to share with you Jesus's victory over death. Jesus made an amazing promise in John 11:25–26: "*I am the resurrection and the life. The one who believes in me will live, even though they die; and whoever lives by believing in me will never die.*"

That's quite a promise! Jesus proved He could do it by rising from the grave. Otherwise, we would have no reason to believe it. If Jesus hadn't died on the cross and risen from the grave, you would have no reason to believe that there was life after death. There would be no hope of the afterlife and no eternal life. The Bible says, however, "*By his power God raised the Lord from the dead, and **he will raise us also***" (1 Corinthians 6:14).

Make a decision to trust Jesus with your life. Follow as a disciple. Run with perseverance the race set before you. (See Hebrews 12:1.)

GRANDFATHER RAN THE RACE

My grandfather was a Baptist preacher. He was a circuit rider, meaning that he had four churches, a different one each weekend of the month. After a season, two of the churches really grew and asked that he preach every other weekend. Finally one church, Bethel Baptist Church, asked him to devote all of his ministry to their congregation. He stayed there for more than forty years.

He died when I was nine. He's now in my "*great cloud of witnesses*" (Hebrews 12:1). I often think about what he would say to me as a pastor. I believe he is looking down on me with love, cheering me on to run a good race.

When I heard the call to be a pastor, the first church I served was Southside Baptist Church. I had known the pastor, Dale Chambliss, since I was a kid, and he brought me on as an intern. On my first day, however, something happened that blew my mind. I arrived in the office and met an associate pastor named Tom Camp.

Tom said, "Brent, you don't know me, but I was in your granddaddy's church growing up. He was a great pastor. Over the years, he lamented that he didn't have more young pastors rise up to be trained for ministry. When I was a teenager, I stepped forward and said I would be a pastor like him. I was the only one in his forty-one years of pastoring. I would have never dreamed that one day I would be serving a church with his grandson."

Tom looked at me and continued, "Now it's your turn. I will do all I can to help you succeed in ministry." From that day forward, he encouraged me, shared ministry lessons, prayed for me, and loved me well, just like my granddaddy would have done.

Jesus has won the victory, but Easter isn't just about Jesus. It's about you and your victory. Christ shares His victory over fear, sin, and death. You can rise, too.

> Since we are surrounded by such a great cloud of witnesses, let us throw off everything that hinders and the sin that so easily entangles. And let us run with perseverance the race marked out for us, fixing our eyes on Jesus, the pioneer and perfecter of faith.   (Hebrews 12:1–2)

Look up to Him today. See Jesus cheering you on. Ask for what you need. Make Him proud. Lean on Him if you're weary. Listen to Him if you don't know where to turn. Run a good race.

PRAYER PRINCIPLE #22:

Faithful prayer lifts up the next generation.

23

SAY PLEASE

*Just as we have been approved by God to be entrusted with
the gospel, so we speak, not to please man, but to please God
who tests our hearts.*
—1 Thessalonians 2:4 (ESV)

My favorite memory of my father involves Dixie Youth Baseball.
Dad was my biggest fan. He always showed up for my games and cheered
in the stands.

On one occasion, when I was around eight years old, I got a big hit to
center field. I headed for first. As I rounded the base, I could see the out-
fielder overthrowing to the second baseman. I dashed for second. Without
thinking, I decided to keep running for third. By this time, the catcher had
the ball and threw to the third baseman. He bobbled the ball, and I saw
my chance. Rounding third, I headed for home, sliding safely under the
catcher's mitt just as he caught the ball.

It was an in-the-park home run. It was one of those moments when I
felt kind of out of my mind. The coach was going nuts. The fans were going
crazy. But my dad's reaction became seared in my memory and always
brings a smile to my face.

Dad came running out onto the field and met me at home plate. I'm sure that wasn't allowed. Like me, he wasn't thinking clearly. Jumping up and down, he had a huge smile on his face and open arms. He was more excited than I was.

If you could have one day back from childhood, what would it be? I would pick that day.

Sons always want to make their fathers happy. We want our fathers to be *"well pleased"* with us. (See Matthew 3:17.)

Sometimes, however, the relationships between sons and fathers can be strained. Sons can carry a lot of anger against their dads. Even though that day on the baseball field was special, I always wished there had been more of them. My dad and I struggled to be close when we weren't at the ball field. Dad passed away in 2006, leaving me with quite a bit of baggage. Even so, to the very end of his life, the impulse to please my father was always strong.

JESUS HAD ONE DRIVING DESIRE: TO PLEASE HIS HEAVENLY FATHER. THAT SHOULD BE OUR DESIRE TOO.

Jesus had one driving desire: to please His heavenly Father. He spoke of His relationship to His Abba—meaning *Father*—in intimate terms. Jesus said:

> *I do nothing on my own but speak just what the Father has taught me. The one who sent me is with me; he has not left me alone, for I always do what pleases him.* (John 8:28–29)

Jesus lived to please God. God was always with Him. In fact, Jesus said, *"Whoever has seen me has seen the Father…Do you not believe that I am in the Father and the Father is in me? The words that I say to you I do not speak on my own authority, but the Father who dwells in me does his works"* (John 14:9–10 ESV).

"IF IT WOULD PLEASE YOU, LORD"

Do you live to please your heavenly Father?

George Müller had a common phrase in his prayers. He would say something along these lines: "If it would please You, Lord." The idea of pleasing God permeated his prayers.

+ February 26, 1842: "My prayer this morning was in particular *that the Lord would be pleased* now to look in pity upon us."

+ December 2, 1835: "This morning I asked the Lord especially that *he would be pleased* to teach me."

+ January 6, 1846: "I am now quietly waiting *the Lord's pleasure.*"

+ December 5, 1850: "Lord, how can thy servant know thy will in this matter? *Wilt thou be pleased to teach him?*"[74]

Toward the end of his life, on a sunny summer day, George Müller was interviewed by a fellow pastor named Charles R. Parsons, who asked Müller about his prayer life, the work of the orphanages, and how God had supplied his needs. Müller's spiritual strength was obvious even at an elderly age.

Parsons asked, "You have always found the Lord faithful to His promise, Mr. Mueller?"

"Always!" Müller declared. "He has never failed me! For nearly seventy years every need in connection with this work has been supplied. The orphans from the first until now have numbered nine thousand five hundred, but they have never wanted a meal. Hundreds of times we have commenced the day without a penny, but our Heavenly Father has sent supplies the moment they were actually required. There never was a time when we had no wholesome meal. During all these years I have been enabled to trust in the living God alone."

Toward the close of the interview, Parsons asked Müller for "a word of special counsel" regarding his own work for God.

---

74. Müller, *The Life of Trust.*

> ## MÜLLER OFFERS THIS SAGE ADVICE: "SEEK TO DEPEND ENTIRELY ON GOD FOR EVERYTHING. PUT YOURSELF AND YOUR WORK INTO HIS HANDS."

Müller answered, "Seek to depend entirely on God for everything. Put yourself and your work into His hands. When thinking of any new undertaking, ask, *Is this agreeable to the mind of God? Is it for His glory?* If it is not for His glory, it is not for your good, and you must have nothing to do with it. Mind that! Having settled that a certain course is for the glory of God, begin it in His name and continue in it to the end. Undertake it in prayer and faith, and never give up!

"And do not regard iniquity in your heart," he continued. "If you do, the Lord will not hear you. Keep that before you always. Then trust in God. Depend only on Him. Wait on Him. Believe on Him. *Expect great things from Him.* Faint not if the blessing tarries. And above all, rely only on the merits of our adorable Lord and Saviour, so that according to them and to nothing of your own, the prayers you offer and the work you do be accepted."[75]

God was pleased to supply Müller with all that he and the orphans needed. Asking God for those needs was not drudgery, but a blessing. Müller wanted to please the Lord through simple faith and prayer.

Faith is pleasing to God.

> *Without faith it is impossible to please him, for whoever would draw near to God must believe that he exists and that he rewards those who seek him.* (Hebrews 11:6 ESV)

There's only one kind of prayer that God answers: the prayer of faith. Matthew 9:29 says, *"According to your faith let it be done to you."* We see so little power in our lives because we exercise so little faith in our lives.

Do you wonder, *What is faith?*

---

75. Charles R. Parsons, "An Hour with George Müller," accessed August 23, 2021, www.lightofword.org/articles/articles-by-george-mueller/225-an-hour-with-george-mueller.

You may say, "I believe God *can* do it!" However, that is not faith. God is able to do what you ask whether you have faith or not. You may also say, "I believe God *might* do it." That isn't faith either. That's hope. However, if you say, "I believe God *will* do it," that's faith. It takes bold faith to pray a prayer like that.

WHEN GOD ANSWERS PRAYERS

Scripture describes the kind of life that leads to believing, prevailing prayer. You can expect that God will answer your prayers when:

+ You live to please only your heavenly Father
+ You trust in God with all of your life
+ You live your life according to God's will
+ You forgive others like Jesus taught
+ You give your life away like Jesus gave His life away
+ You make God your delight
+ You ask in faith

Your prayer is only as powerful as your life. Living in a way that brought pleasure to God, Jesus saw remarkable answers to prayer every day.

Do you live to please Him?

Start today.

You could start with your prayers. Begin to incorporate Müller's phrase into your requests: "If it would please You, Lord…"

You could also begin with your schedule. I often jot down notes when I have time in the morning with God. I list names that come to mind, people to call later that day. I think about events coming up and ask for God's help in meetings and counseling. I also ask God to help me do the things that please Him the most.

Here's a big prayer: Ask, "God, does my work please You? Are the ways I spend most of my days, including the way that I gain income, pleasing to You?" If you wonder if it pleases the Lord, ask how God could recalibrate the way you work or give you a new work that would be more pleasing to the Lord. God's work through you is always about the gospel working in the world. You aren't here to please people. You were made to please God.

Ultimately, as followers of Jesus, we should aspire to imitate Jesus's words regarding the Father: *"I always do what pleases him"* (John 8:29).

God delights in you. So delight in God.

It puts a smile on God's face.

PRAYER PRINCIPLE #23:

Your prayer is only as powerful as your life.

24

AN AUDIENCE WITH
THE KING

*Let us then approach God's throne of grace with confidence, so that
we may receive mercy and find grace to help us in our time of need.*
—Hebrews 4:16

By all accounts, President Abraham Lincoln's youngest son Thomas,
nicknamed "Tad," was a rambunctious boy who had the run of the White
House. Yet he had a soft spot for animals and the downtrodden. It was
Tad's idea to get his father to pardon a turkey that had been given to them
for their Christmas feast. And until his father got wind of what he was
doing, Tad charged visitors a nickel to see Lincoln—but only so he could
donate the money the United States Sanitary Commission, a private relief
agency like the Red Cross.[76]

When Tad was eleven, during the first year of the Civil War, several
men from Kentucky needed to see the president and had been unable to do
so. One day after waiting in the lobby for several hours, they were about

---

76. Gilbert King, "The History of Pardoning Turkeys Began With Tad Lincoln,"
Smithsonian Magazine, November 21, 2012, www.smithsonianmag.com/history/the-
history-of-pardoning-turkeys-began-with-tad-lincoln-141137570.

to give up and mentioned how disappointed they were that they could not see "old Abe." Tad overheard them and rushed to his father's office. "Papa, may I introduce some friends to you?" he asked. President Lincoln agreed, so Tad went back to the men and led them to his father. It was the same group that Lincoln had deliberately been avoiding all week. Later, Lincoln expressed pleasure at his son's diplomacy but had to ask Tad why he called the men his friends.

> "Well," said Tad, "I had seen them so often, and they looked so good and sorry, and said they were from Kentucky, that I thought they must be our friends." To which his father replied, "That is right, my son. I would have the whole human race your friends and mine, if it were possible."[77]

Those Kentuckians received access to Lincoln through his son.

According to the New Testament, in an even more amazing way, you have access to God through His Son, Jesus. Paul writes, "Through him we both [Jew and Gentile] have access to the Father by one Spirit" (Ephesians 2:18).

Every day, you have access to your heavenly Father to ask for what you need. You come to God as a dearly loved child. God is also the King of Kings with overflowing resources. He waits for you to seek an audience with Him, inviting you to ask for what you need, whether it be a physical, mental, emotional, financial, or relational need.

GOD WAITS FOR YOU TO SEEK AN AUDIENCE WITH HIM, INVITING YOU TO ASK FOR WHAT YOU NEED.

If an earthly father who is loving and kind sees his young children approach him with a need, the father will do his best to provide it. How much more so with God?

---

77. Ward Hill Lamon, *Recollections of Abraham Lincoln 1847-1865*, www.gutenberg. org/files/39630/39630-h/39630-h.htm.

Unfortunately, many believers don't approach God with confidence, if they approach at all. They don't depend on God for their every need, look to God in times of trouble, or seek God's face when a decision or crisis comes.

They forget the high price that Jesus paid for such access.

A DONOR RICH IN FAITH

One of the joys of George Müller's ministry was interacting with donors who were also seeking to follow the Lord's will. In his first years in Bristol, England, Müller met a woman with the initials A. L., who lived on a sustenance income. Needlework was her trade, but it brought in very little. She was frail, unable to work long hours, and poor.

After Müller established his first orphanage, the woman's father died, and she inherited a very large sum of money. Despite having a large savings, the father had been a heavy drinker and passed away with great debt. As creditors began lining up, the woman and her siblings had to decide what to do about the debt.

Her brother and two sisters offered to pay the creditors 25 percent of the debt, which was gladly accepted since there was no legal claim on the children. But A. L. thought to herself, "However sinful my father may have been, yet he was my father, and as I have the means of paying his debts to the full amount, I ought, as a believing child, to do so, seeing that my brother and sisters will not do it." So she paid the creditors secretly.

Her siblings then gave some of their money to their mother. But A. L. thought, "I am a child of God; surely I ought to give my mother twice as much as my brothers and sisters." Which is what she did.

Finally, A. L. gave one hundred pounds for the orphan house. The gift surprised Müller. Up to that point, he thought she was quite destitute. He talked with her about the donation and ensured that she wasn't making a rash, emotional decision. Müller found her to be "a quiet, calm, considerate follower of the Lord Jesus." She said she believed the words of Jesus when He said, *"Lay not up for yourselves treasures upon earth"* (Matthew 6:19 KJV) and *"Sell that thou hast, and give to the poor"* (Matthew 19:21 KJV).

When Müller asked her if she had truly "counted the cost" (see Luke 14:28) in giving the large sum, she answered, "The Lord Jesus has given his last drop of blood for me, and should I not give him this hundred pounds?"[78]

Jesus gave a precious gift—His life and His blood—so that you can have access to God. Then why delay in taking your every need to your heavenly Father?

Like George Müller and A. L., my grandmother took her every need to the Lord. I can remember hearing her pray. Her prayers were simple but powerful; each day, she asked for what she needed. She was not rich in money but was rich in faith.

REMAINING CALM IN A STORM

Every summer, I would visit my grandmother in Mobile, Alabama. She had a little clapboard home on Mobile Bay, where I loved to swim and fish. Storms would blow through often, and some of them were very strong. I was seven years old when a tropical storm headed toward Mobile. I remember the family's conversation of whether to stay or go, flee or ride it out. The adults decided to ride it out. They shuttered the windows and tied everything down.

I will never forget that night. The wind was howling. That little wooden house was literally shaking. The lights went out, and the thunder sounded like a freight train. Lightning landed in the front yard. I was terrified and didn't sleep a wink.

After the storm, trees were down and shingles were scattered everywhere, but that little house was still standing.

My grandmother was confident and calm through all of it. She was concerned, but did not panic. Her faith kept her steady as she kept her eyes on God, not the storm.

That experience makes me think about what Jesus said about a wise builder:

Everyone who hears these words of mine and puts them into practice
is like a wise man who built his house on the rock. The rain came

---

78. Müller, *The Life of Trust.*

down, the streams rose, and the winds blew and beat against that
house; yet it did not fall, because it had its foundation on the rock.

(Matthew 7:24–25)

WHEN THE RAINS OF HARDSHIP, THE WINDS OF SADNESS, AND THE STORMS OF STRUGGLE COME, A LIFE BUILT ON JESUS WON'T FALL DOWN.

Jesus, His teachings, and His life are our Rock. Life on the Rock of Jesus means complete dependence on Him. When the rains of hardship, the winds of sadness, and the storms of struggle come, a life built on Him won't fall down. But the foolish person who builds their life on shifting sands—on self-reliance, money, possessions, school grades, accomplishments, or career experience—will find it collapsing when the rains come and the winds blow.

It's a question of trust. In whom or what do you trust? Many people don't know these days. They're not sure if they trust religious leaders, who sometimes have a reputation for being all about money, power, and control. People don't know if they can trust the news. Is it biased or even false? Who can be believed? Can this politician be trusted? What about this doctor or this lawyer? Can the stock market be trusted?

Distrust is a growing epidemic. But you can't have peace unless you know what you can depend on. When the storm comes, you realize whether you've built your life on something solid or something that sinks. What you trust is ultimately where you'll invest your time, your mental energy, and your financial resources.

We put our trust in things and people every day. Whenever you fly, you are surrendering to the pilot in a way. You just have to sit there and trust. You can't do anything to make the plane take off or land. When you undergo general anesthesia for a medical procedure, you put your trust in the doctors to do the right thing.

Everyone needs help. Everyone needs something steady to stand on. Your life patterns and how you hold up in a storm always reveal what you really trust.

GOD WAITS TO BLESS YOU

God says, *"I know the plans I have for you...plans to prosper you and not to harm you, plans to give you hope and a future"* (Jeremiah 29:11). God has good things in store for you. He is not waiting to condemn you. God is there to bless you, love you, and take you into His arms and say, "I forgive you. I want to help you. I'm here. Come to My throne, and you'll find mercy."

When you go to that throne, you can't hold anything back. If you're not moving toward total reliance and trust, you won't experience the fullness of God's peace and protection. You won't find the steadiness that comes from leaning on the Rock of Ages.

What steps do you need to take to build your life on the rock?

Where are you lacking in confidence?

Are there prayers you gave up on years ago, believing that somehow God had not heard?

You may not have access to a president, but the King of the universe wants to hear from you. Go to God with your needs now.

This is the confidence we have in approaching God: that if we ask anything according to his will, he hears us. (1 John 5:14)

Go confidently.

Receive mercy and grace.

PRAYER PRINCIPLE #24:

God rewards confident, bold prayers.

25

GIVE IT A TRY

My God, my God, why have you forsaken me?
—Matthew 27:46

One of the lowest points of my life happened about seventeen years ago. My father had died after a prolonged illness. I had just taken a new ministry position. Within a few weeks of starting the job, I realized it was going to be a difficult season. I thought I could help to turn it around, but after two years, I realized that my own soul was in crisis.

For the first time in my life, I experienced depression. Unfamiliar with what depression felt like, I had no frame of reference. I struggled to sleep, and it was hard to concentrate. I was unhappy in normal situations and suffered from occasional panic attacks. It was a scary time as my emotions seemed very far outside my control.

My spiritual struggle was intense. Feeling abandoned, I wondered why God had forsaken me. I had given my life to God. I was trying to please Him. My thoughts revealed a false but deeply held belief that if I served the Lord, I would be immune from suffering.

TROUBLES ARE INEVITABLE

Jesus warned us that suffering is inevitable, saying, *"In this world you will have trouble"* (John 16:33). That truth entered my life on a level I had never experienced before. I had trouble praying and feeling connected to God. From time to time, I look back over the entries of a journal I kept from those days. I'm amazed at what I poured out before the Lord—frustration, anger, disappointment, doubt.

Just when I thought I couldn't go any lower, I met the living God. God had not abandoned me after all. Little by little, God lifted me out of that pit. My family and friends helped. I began to feel hope. I got help. I got better. I started to experience God's love on a deeper level. Today, I can relate to those who struggle with depression and the heaviness of grief.

Some people wonder if God really knows what we go through in this life.

Yes, He does.

The Messiah, Jesus, came into the world as a helpless babe and grew into a Man who was *"despised and rejected—a man of sorrows, acquainted with deepest grief"* (Isaiah 53:3 NLT). Jesus entered into the suffering of this life. Willing to endure the worst this life can give, He knows what we feel.

On the cross, Jesus felt forsaken at His earthly life's lowest point—one much lower than mine.

He cried, *"My God, my God, why have you forsaken me?"* (Matthew 27:46).

A doctrine called divine abandonment says that God the Father abandoned Jesus when He was on the cross. Because Jesus had taken all the sin of the world upon Himself, God turned away in that moment.

The idea that God had turned His back on Jesus was so troubling to Martin Luther, the father of the Protestant Reformation, that it caused Luther to go into seclusion to try to understand it. He came away as confused as when he started. He couldn't understand where God was relative to Jesus on the cross—much like I struggled to know where God was when I went through the dark night of the soul.

> **THERE WAS NEVER A MOMENT WHEN JESUS CEASED TO BE THE SON OF GOD. THERE WAS NEVER A TIME WHEN GOD DIDN'T SUFFER WITH HIM.**

I don't deny that Jesus felt forsaken. But I don't believe He was abandoned. There was never a moment when He ceased to be the Son of God. There was never a time when God didn't suffer with Him. In the moment of His intense trial, it may be that Jesus felt forsaken because the weight of sin caused Him to lose intimacy with God.

Intimacy with God was the fuel of Jesus's earthly journey. It gave Him energy, comforted Him in grief, provided power for miracles, and sustained Him in His mission.

In dying for us, Jesus made a way for us to know God intimately, too. We can be healed because of His sacrifice. As Peter explained:

> *He himself bore our sins in his body on the tree, that we might die to sin and live to righteousness. By his wounds you have been healed.*
>
> (1 Peter 2:24 ESV)

READY TO ANSWER OUR PRAYERS

George Müller's life demonstrates that we can be richly and deeply connected to our heavenly Father. Even in low moments, Müller sensed that God was there to sustain him. He knew that such care from his heavenly Father was a gracious gift. He wrote:

> Dear reader, do not think that I have attained in faith (and how much less in other respects) to that degree to which I might and ought to attain; but thank God for the faith that He has given to me. Please pray that He will uphold and increase it. Finally, once more, I remind you not to let Satan deceive you in making you think that you could not have the same faith, but that it is only for persons who are in a similar situation as I.[79]

---

79. Müller, *Release the Power of Prayer*, 39.

Müller goes on to describe what that intimacy with God looks like. When he lost a key, he asked God to help him find it. When someone was late for an appointment with him, Müller, feeling inconvenienced, would ask the Lord to hasten the person's arrival. When he didn't understand a passage of Scripture, he asked that God would be pleased by the Holy Spirit to teach him the meaning. He wanted other believers to pray to the Lord in the same way, writing:

> Oh, I beseech you, do not think that I am an extraordinary believer, having privileges above any other of God's dear children, which they cannot have. Do not look on my way of acting as something that would not work for other believers. Give it a try! Stand still in the hour of trial, and you will see the help of God, if you trust in Him.[80]

Jesus's heartfelt cry of *"My God, my God, why have you forsaken me?"* was not the last thing He said on the cross. His final cry was, *"It is finished"* (John 19:30). The work of bringing salvation to lost humanity was done. God helped Jesus complete all that Jesus came to do.

When have you felt forsaken by God?

Do you feel forsaken now?

GOD DOES NOT ABANDON YOU IN A SEASON OF DARKNESS. WHAT SEEMS LIKE DEFEAT CAN BECOME YOUR DELIVERANCE.

Jesus was not forsaken in His great suffering. I was not abandoned in my season of darkness.

Neither are you. What seems like defeat can become your deliverance. The valley becomes the place where you encounter God like never before.

---

80. Ibid., 40.

TWO WAYS TO PRAY IN HARD SEASONS

When you feel forsaken, here are two ways to pray:

- First, pour out your heart. Hold nothing back before the Lord. Have faith that even if you feel abandoned, forsaken, or lost, your heavenly Father is still present, and you are none of those things. Keep a journal of your journey through grief and pain. Write out your raw prayers and let them go before God. Ask for a fresh expression of God's love.

- Second, take God at His word. Surround yourself with Scripture. Pray God's Word.

GOD'S PROMISES IN HIS WORD

Here are just a few of God's promises that you can use in prayer:

Fear not, for I am with you; be not dismayed, for I am your God; I will strengthen you, I will help you, I will uphold you with my righteous right hand. (Isaiah 41:10 ESV)

God is with you when you're afraid. God knows when you're discouraged and need His strength.

Have I not commanded you? Be strong and courageous. Do not be afraid; do not be discouraged, for the LORD your God will be with you wherever you go. (Joshua 1:9)

God hasn't abandoned you, even when you feel that God is absent.

It is the LORD who goes before you. He will be with you; he will not leave you or forsake you. Do not fear or be dismayed. (Deuteronomy 31:8 ESV)

God will never leave. God goes in front of you as you walk a hard road.

For I am convinced that neither death nor life, neither angels nor demons, neither the present nor the future, nor any powers, neither height nor depth, nor anything else in all creation, will be able

to separate us from the love of God that is in Christ Jesus our Lord.
(Romans 8:38–39)

God's love will never let you go. Nothing can separate you from God's love. Not physical problems, not emotional problems, not relational problems, not career problems, not mental problems—nothing.

And we know that in all things God works for the good of those who love him, who have been called according to his purpose.
(Romans 8:28)

For many years, Sarah Young, the author of *Jesus Calling*, suffered with infections related to Lyme disease. Each day, she faced chronic dizziness and constant discouragement. But she kept getting up to pray and write. She said:

If I had been healthier I would not have been able to write this book. It chronicles my journey from discouragement to hope. There seems to be a sense of hopelessness creeping into many people's mindsets as they look at problems in their lives and in world events. But the hope we can find in the Bible is a sturdy reality—no matter what is happening in our lives or in the world.[81]

God is working for your good. Whatever brings you closer to God is a good thing, even if it feels like a bad thing.

Believe God's Word. Look for God's help. Don't be afraid. Trust that God is working for good, no matter what you're going through. God is with you.

PRAYER PRINCIPLE #25:

Whatever brings you closer to God is a good thing.

---

81. Andy Butcher, "Sarah Young: Amid Suffering, Devotion," *Publisher's Weekly*, November 14, 2012, accessed August 23, 2021, www.publishersweekly.com/pw/by-topic/industry-news/religion/article/54756-sarah-young-amid-suffering-devotion.html.

26

A PRAYER FOR
A DECK CHAIR

When you pray, do not keep on babbling like pagans, for they think
they will be heard because of their many words. Do not be like
them, for your Father knows what you need before you ask him.
—Matthew 6:7–8

In 1974, Steve McQueen was the highest paid movie star in the world, receiving $12 million for *The Towering Inferno*. Nicknamed "the King of Cool," Steve made movies like *Bullitt*, *The Great Escape*, and *The Magnificent Seven*. Dashing and confident, he was the definition of a self-made man.

Sadly, Steve suffered a horrific childhood of neglect and abuse. His father abandoned his mother soon after Steve was born. When he was three years old, she left him with her parents, then reclaimed him five years later. She married, divorced, and married again. Both stepfathers beat him. Out on the streets at age nine, Steve soon became involved in local gangs and even worked at a brothel.

After a series of odd jobs and three years of service in the U.S. Marine Corps, Steve took acting classes, worked in theater, and had a small part in a movie. Eventually he became the most popular movie star not only in America, but globally.

Steve once said that he often had nightmares that everything he had gained could suddenly be taken away from him. A man of paradoxes, he was both humble and defiant, stingy and generous, gentle and violent, self-assured and insecure. One of his directors said, "He was a loner, and he was troubled, and he was looking for a father."

Living for himself, Steve answered to no one. Once asked if he believed in God, the actor replied, "I believe in me. God will be number one as long as I'm number one." He had all the money, cars, alcohol, drugs, and women that a man could ever want. It was only a matter of time before he became addicted in every way. Substance abuse, serial womanizing, jealousy, and violence—Steve did it all.

AN AIRBORNE MINISTRY

By 1979, he felt empty. He moved away from Hollywood, bought a plane, and learned how to fly. Steve spent a lot of time with his flying instructor, a humble, grumpy Christian named Sammy Mason. As they shared long hours in the air talking about the meaning of life, Steve sensed something different about Mason. The more time they spent together, the more Steve wanted to know Mason's secret. One day, Mason told him about his relationship with Jesus Christ. Steve began to attend Mason's church, sitting in the balcony section for several months. One day, he asked to meet with the pastor, Leonard Dewitt. Steve had a lot of questions— and he told Dewitt that he had become a born-again Christian.

The "King of Cool" had met the King of the universe, Jesus Christ. The change in Steve was "dramatic," Mason said. "I doubt that I have ever seen a man flourish with more spiritual reality in such a short time."[82] For the first time in his life, Steve knew that he was blessed by his heavenly Father.

Unfortunately, he had only been a Christian for a short time when he was diagnosed with terminal cancer. He wanted more than anything to meet Billy Graham. Four days before Steve's death, the evangelist visited

82. Esther O'Reilly, "Greater Grace: A Story of God, Redemption, and Steve McQueen," *Patheos*, December 9, 2012, www.patheos.com/blogs/youngfogey/2012/12/greater-grace-a-story-of-god-redemption-and-steve-mcqueen.

him in the hospital. After they prayed together, Graham gave Steve his own Bible, which he signed with the message, "To my friend Steve McQueen, may God bless and keep you always."

Steve died on November 7, 1980—Graham's sixty-second birthday—clutching that Bible.[83] It was opened to his favorite verse:

> *For God so loved the world, that he gave his only begotten Son, that whosoever believeth in him should not perish, but have everlasting life.*
>
> (John 3:16 KJV)

That truth changed Steve's life. Before he died, he experienced total forgiveness of his sins. He had found a Father.

God wants nothing more than for you to know Him as a good Father. You may have had a bad father, a distant father, or a harsh father; but Jesus said that God is a *good* Father who *"knows what you need before you ask him"* (Matthew 6:8). Jesus called God *Abba*, which means *Daddy*.

Jesus said, *"This, then, is how you should pray: 'Our Father in heaven…'"* (Matthew 6:9). Jesus was born into a Jewish religious system, but in all of the Old Testament, there is not one prayer to God that begins with *Father*. However, *every* prayer Jesus prayed began with the word "Father" except for the one during His passion in which He cried out, *"My God"* (Matthew 27:46). Yet even from the cross, Jesus prayed, *"Father, forgive them, for they do not know what they are doing"* (Luke 23:34). In His dying moments, Jesus forgave all who tortured Him, called for His death, or turned a blind eye.

IF WE PRAY LIKE JESUS DID, WE WILL LOOK TO AND TRUST OUR HEAVENLY FATHER IN ALL CIRCUMSTANCES, BIG AND SMALL.

What allowed Him to pray that prayer? Where did He find the strength and grace to pray such a prayer? If we could answer those questions, maybe

83. "The Moment Steve McQueen's Life Changed," Billy Graham Evangelistic Association, September 26, 2017, billygraham.org/story/moment-steve-mcqueens-life-changed.

we could learn to forgive. Maybe we could have peace even when we are falsely accused or wronged without cause. Maybe we could pray like Jesus did, always looking to and trusting our heavenly Father in all circumstances, big and small.

WAITING FOR A CHAIR FROM GOD

Just before setting sail from Quebec to Liverpool on the steamship *Sardinian* in June 1880, George Müller had a problem. A deck chair for Mrs. Müller had not yet arrived from New York. A fellow passenger, evangelist and hymn writer D. W. Whittle, suggested that Müller purchase another at a nearby shop. Müller replied:

> No, my brother, Our Heavenly Father will send the chair from New York. It is one used by Mrs. Müller, as we came over, and left in New York when we landed. I wrote ten days ago to a brother who promised to see it forwarded here last week. He has not been prompt as I would have desired, but I am sure Our Heavenly Father will send the chair. Mrs. Müller is very sick upon the sea, and has particularly desired to have this same chair, and not finding it here yesterday when we arrived, as we expected, we have made special prayer that Our Heavenly Father would be pleased to provide it for us, and we will trust Him to do so.[84]

Müller waited peacefully on the tender craft even though he could have easily purchased another chair for a few dollars. Just as the craft was about to leave the dock to take the passengers to the *Sardinian*, a wagon drove up—and on top of the load was Mrs. Müller's chair. "The Lord having a lesson for me," Whittle later recalled, it was placed in Whittle's hands.

Müller took the chair "with the happy, pleased expression of a child who has just received a kindness deeply appreciated, and reverently removing his hat and folding his hands over it, he thanked his Heavenly Father for sending the chair."[85]

---

84. "God Brought a Chair in Answer to Prayer," taken from D. W. Whittle's *The Wonders of Prayer*, accessed August 23, 2021, www.georgemuller.org/devotional/god-brought-a-chair-in-answer-to-prayer5277958.
85. Ibid.

Nothing is too great or small to bring before your heavenly Father. *"Cast all your anxiety on him because he cares for you"* (1 Peter 5:7).

In his hour of need for salvation, Steve McQueen cried out to God. Even when near death, he trusted his heavenly Father. When he needed a Bible for comfort and assurance, his heavenly Father provided one, from none other than Billy Graham.

> **THE SIMPLE YET ASTOUNDING TRUTH IS THAT GOD CARES FOR US AS A HEAVENLY FATHER WHO LOVES TO HEAR AND ANSWER OUR PRAYERS.**

We may think that we need to impress God with our lengthy, pious prayers. We may think that God can't be bothered with our tedious needs. We may fail to believe the simple yet astounding truth that God cares for us as a heavenly Father and loves to hear and answer our prayers. We cannot imagine that Jesus's words are actually true: *"Ask and it will be given to you…If you… know how to give good gifts to your children, how much more will your Father in heaven give good gifts to those who ask him!"* (Matthew 7:7, 11).

Perhaps we need to be like the disciples who cried out to the Lord, *"Increase our faith!"* (Luke 17:5)

Talk to God today like a child to a father. Ask for what you need. Believe in the simple reliance that God will supply your need.

PRAYER PRINCIPLE #26:

Your heavenly Father will help you, no matter how large or small the need.

27

EARNEST PRAYERS

*Therefore I tell you, whatever you ask for in prayer, believe that you
have received it, and it will be yours.*
—Mark 11:24

When we moved from Dallas, Texas, to Knoxville, Tennessee, my
wife Jen and I had an opportunity to put believing prayer into practice.

Ten years beforehand, as we moved from Birmingham, Alabama, to
Dallas, we tried to sell our home in the wake of the 2008 recession. After
a few months, we felt a little discouraged. When a year had passed and the
home still had not sold, we began to really worry. At the two-year mark,
panic started to set in as we wondered if we would just have to walk away
and experience foreclosure. We had never faced such a decision as a married couple and felt the weight of breaking a contract with our signatures.
Two years and four months after we listed the home, we finally sold it for
less than what we had originally paid. It felt awful.

But God is good. We knew we were called to Dallas. In our ten years
in Texas, we met so many wonderful people and saw God's hand at work
again and again. Both Jen and I grew in dependence on prayer and faith.
We experienced growth in our personal prayer lives.

BELIEVING FOR A QUICK SALE

The calling to Knoxville felt just as sure. I confess, however, that the prospect of selling our home in Dallas brought back bad memories of sleepless nights and dwindling savings. The possibility of once again losing money, while not being able to fully embrace our new home, created great anxiety as we prepared to move to Knoxville. Committed to praying together and individually for a quick sale, we believed in faith that our house would sell in short order.

Daily we asked God that our home would sell at the price we had in mind. Jen and I would pause and pray together whenever we had a home showing alert. We waited and waited. Weeks went by with multiple showings. Some potential buyers came back for a second look but made no offers. Finally, one Friday after a week of frustration, I felt dispirited and prayed, "God, I am asking in faith that we will have an offer by Sunday." I believed that we would.

On Saturday, we had a showing and the same family came back the next day. They expressed an interest that suggested that they would make an offer. No offer came on Sunday. Or the next day. Or the next.

I wondered what had happened. Had I not prayed with sufficient faith? Had I been presumptive with God, too demanding, wanting God to act on my timetable?

Strangely, however, I wasn't worried. I felt like the second showing and at least the prospect of an offer were signs from God. It was as though God was saying, "I am with you, and I am working. Don't be discouraged. Keep praying and trusting." The second showing was like a little deposit on a promise that God was going to fulfill.

I am learning that sometimes God works this way in prayer. I might pray and wait for something, believing God will bring it about, but it only occurs in God's timing. It doesn't happen when *I* want it to happen. Through God's mercy and great love for me and my family, however, God encourages our faith with small signs that our prayer will be answered in a large way. This reality has been apparent in countless ways as Jen and I pray for our children, extended family, friends, and everyday needs.

GOD TAKES PLEASURE IN OUR PERSISTENCE IN PRAYER. HE ISN'T PUT OFF WHEN WE ASK FOR HELP AGAIN AND AGAIN.

God delights in being asked to provide for us in prayer. He takes pleasure in our persistence in prayer. God isn't put off when we ask for help again and again. In fact, Jesus taught that sometimes we must pray repeatedly to see the miracle come about.

> *Keep on asking, and you will receive what you ask for. Keep on seeking, and you will find. Keep on knocking, and the door will be opened to you. For everyone who asks, receives. Everyone who seeks, finds. And to everyone who knocks, the door will be opened.*
>
> (Matthew 7:7–8 NLT)

Persistence pays off. The gift will be given, the item sought will be found, and the door will be opened.

We may think that such gifts and discoveries will be achieved or such doors will be opened in an instant. But what if God answers prayer in deposits and guarantees until all is fulfilled? What if the walk of faith and simple reliance on God matters more than the actual prayer being answered?

God has given the Holy Spirit to us as a sign that one day we will be completely renewed in Christ. *"He has identified us as his own by placing the Holy Spirit in our hearts as the first installment that guarantees everything he has promised us"* (2 Corinthians 1:22 nlt).

A similar spiritual dynamic is at work when we pray.

WAITING ON THE LORD

George Müller often found himself waiting for his prayer to be answered. He might pray for ten pounds for the day's expenses and rejoice when a smaller amount, like five shillings, was given because it showed him that God was moving for his good and the good of the orphans under Müller's care.

In 1845, when he began to ask God daily for 10,000 pounds for the building of the first orphan house, Müller prayed for thirty-five consecutive days and did not receive a single shilling. Nevertheless, he comforted himself with words from James 1:2–4, especially God's teaching, *"Let perseverance finish its work"* (James 1:4). Müller asked God to increase his faith and sustain his patience.

On the thirty-sixth day, December 10, 1845, he received 1,000 pounds toward the new building. Müller recounts that he was as calm and quiet as if he had only received one shilling. Day by day, he was *expecting* an answer to his prayer. He was looking for God's supply. Therefore, the donation didn't surprise him.[86]

Three days later, he received no funds, but a promise from an unknown Christian architect that drawings for the new home would be freely offered.

On day fifty, nothing more had been given. It would be understandable if Müller had thought, *God, why did You send this money but no more? Why would You only give a small amount when so much is required?*

However, Müller wrote:

This morning I have been particularly encouraged by the consideration that the Lord has sent me the one thousand pounds, and the promise from that pious architect, whom I have never seen, and of whose name I am as yet in ignorance, *not to mock me, but as an earnest that he will give all that is needed.*[87]

Perhaps more than any other teaching on prayer from George Müller, this concept of *earnest* prayers has been revolutionary for my life. It helps me look out for small answers to prayer and give thanks when they come. It allows me to stay steady in faith even when it seems that little is happening.

WHEN WE PRAY IN EARNEST, WE CAN WATCH FOR SMALL ANSWERS TO PRAYER AND GIVE THANKS WHEN THEY COME.

86. Müller, *The Life of Trust.*
87. Ibid.

What might this mean for your life?

It may mean that when you pray for years for a prodigal son or daughter to come home, you can rejoice when a godly friend comes into their life.

It could mean that when you pray for God to supply a way to embark on a new career path—one you believe He desires for you—you can rejoice when a new contact is made or an avenue opens to see the dream fulfilled.

It may mean that when you ask God for help in being reconciled to a family member, you can rejoice when at least a small sign of reconnection or forgiveness is given.

As we tried to sell our home in Dallas, on the Monday evening after Sunday's disappointment, I gave God thanks for the strong interest that had been shown in our home. I asked God again to sell our home quickly.

Two days later, we had an offer of exactly the amount we sought.

Prayer doesn't always work that way. Sometimes it takes two years and four months to see a prayer answered. Sometimes it takes only a few weeks. Along the way, however, you can expect that God will reveal in small and big ways that *He hears and is moving.*

Brothers and sisters, don't give up. Keep believing that God has heard your prayers. Keep asking again and again in faith. Look for deposits on the fulfillment of those prayers.

The apostle Paul wrote, *"My God will meet all your needs according to the riches of his glory in Christ Jesus"* (Philippians 4:19).

You can take that to the bank.

PRAYER PRINCIPLE #27:

God makes small deposits on big answers to prayer.

28

TREES WALKING AROUND

Truly I tell you, if you have faith as small as a mustard seed, you can say to this mountain, "Move from here to there," and it will move. Nothing will be impossible for you.
—Matthew 17:20

When I was in Israel in 2017, our group walked through the ruins of Bethsaida along the Sea of Galilee. This is the village where Peter grew up. Enough of a shell of the first-century village remains today so that one can imagine meandering through the narrow streets and entering *oikos* (extended household) dwellings. We could also see the ruins of the village gate, a singular passage to let residents in and keep strangers and enemies out.

Something remarkable happened outside the Bethsaida gate, both for a first-century man and for me.

The eighth chapter of the Gospel of Mark tells of a time when Jesus entered Bethsaida. Some people brought forward a blind man and begged

Jesus to heal him. Jesus led him by the hand outside the gate, then spit on the man's eyes and placed His hands on him.

> Jesus asked, "Do you see anything?" He looked up and said, "I see people; they look like trees walking around." Once more Jesus put his hands on the man's eyes. Then his eyes were opened, his sight was restored, and he saw everything clearly. (Mark 8:23–25)

Outside the Bethsaida gate, our guide recounted the story of what had happened there nearly two thousand years beforehand. Then he asked, "Does anyone want to receive prayer for healing today?"

I grew up not really believing in healing. That is to say, I believed it was possible because I believe in Jesus, but I didn't *really* believe in it. I thought prayer for healing didn't happen today, or if it did, it occurred only rarely or for the super-spiritual.

RECEIVING PRAYER FOR HEALING

When the guide asked if anyone wanted to receive prayer for healing, I surprised myself when I impulsively said, "I do."

From around the age of ten, I had suffered from acid reflux so badly that sometimes I had to go to the emergency room. After about a decade of consistent discomfort, I began to take a proton pump inhibitor (PPI) such as Prilosec or Nexium. It was like a miracle drug although I had to keep increasing the dosage for relief.

Just before my trip to Israel, I had read that PPIs were linked to memory issues in senior adults. Because I had been taking them for such a long time, my doctor advised that I wean off of them. That was on my mind as I traveled.

The Holy Land has a way of generating faith. Seeing the places where Jesus walked, imagining the miracles, wanting to trust Jesus more—all contributed to a spiritual high that I felt in Israel.

SEEING THE PLACES WHERE JESUS WALKED, IMAGINING THE MIRACLES, AND WANTING TO TRUST JESUS MORE ALL HAVE A WAY OF GENERATING FAITH.

It was a leap of faith for me to say, "I want a prayer for healing."

I described my long-term problem and how I wanted to be healed. For several minutes, the group prayed over me and placed their hands on my stomach. Then the guide asked, "How do you feel? Do you sense anything different?"

Though it was faint, I could feel something different in my abdomen. I believed something real had happened. Full of faith, I stopped taking my PPI that night. I felt fine the next day and then the next.

Three weeks later, after we returned home, my acid reflux returned with a vengeance. I was a bit discouraged, but I clung to the belief that healing had indeed come to me. I thought, "I don't want to get back on a PPI. Maybe the next step of faith is to see a doctor." I'm embarrassed that after suffering for thirty years, I was finally considering the idea of seeing a specialist.

In addition to being a very good physician, my specialist was a follower of Jesus. When I arrived for my first appointment, all he wanted to talk about was theology. I get that a lot as a pastor. However, all I wanted to talk about was my stomach. He ran some tests and referred me to a surgeon for a radical new procedure using a series of magnets in a bracelet around the esophagus.

Within a month, I had the surgery. The recovery was more difficult than expected, but over time, I began feeling more like myself and started eating in a regular way. Unlike before, I didn't worry about acidic or spicy foods.

After thirty years of suffering, I can say that God healed me.

My healing didn't happen in a miraculous way. It wasn't a complete change in an instant. But it was a miracle, and I was healed.

Some people receive healing with a word. Other people are healed over time. In my case, God used a trip to Israel, the prayer of a faithful community, and two doctors.

Along the way, God increased my faith. After the Israel pilgrimage, I increased time in Bible study and prayer each day. My goal was to walk in faith even if the full miracle hadn't happened yet.

EXPECT ANSWERS TO PRAYER

One theme throughout Müller's book *Release the Power of Prayer* is that his experience with answered prayer is not unique. Even though Müller celebrated over 50,000 answered prayers, he never thought that he had the "gift" of faith (see 1 Corinthians 12:9) or believed his faith to be extraordinary.

Müller sought to depend on God moment by moment. This kind of life is available to every believer, Müller argued. God wants all of His children to pray in all things, cast their burdens on Him (see Psalm 55:22), and enjoy the full benefits of a loving, benevolent Father.

Müller wrote, "In all of my temporal and spiritual concerns, I pray to the Lord and expect an answer to my requests. May you not do the same, dear believing reader?"[88]

GOD WANTS US TO GROW IN BELIEF SO THAT WE WON'T FORSAKE HIM IN THE HOUR OF TRIAL, BUT INSTEAD TURN TO HIM, ASK FOR WHAT IS NEEDED, AND THEN WAIT IN FAITH.

Faith is the key. God wants us to grow in belief so that we won't forsake Him in the hour of trial, but instead turn to Him, ask for what is needed, and then wait in faith.

---

88. Müller, *Release the Power of Prayer*, 40.

FOUR KEYS TO AN INCREASE OF FAITH

Müller notes that an increase of faith is a good gift that comes from God and believers should ask for this blessing.[89] He suggests four essential means for this to occur:

1. "The careful reading of the word of God, combined with meditation on it." This will provide believers "with a measure of confidence to rely upon him."

Outside the Bethsaida gate, we reflected on the story of the blind man who was healed. We wouldn't have access to that story apart from God's Word.

The Bible teaches us something about God's character and nature. We learn how loving, good, gracious, and generous God is. We read stories of how people endured all kinds of hardship, fatigue, famines, and failures. God proved faithful through all those experiences.

Meditating on God's Word strengthens faith.

2. "The believer should not shrink from situations, positions, circumstances, in which his faith may be tried, but should cheerfully embrace them as opportunities where he may see the hand of God stretched out on his behalf, to help and deliver him."

Like a muscle, faith is strengthened when put under stress.

In his journal, Müller wrote, "The more I am in a position to be tried in faith with reference to my body, my family, my service for the Lord, my business, etc., the more shall I have opportunity of seeing God's help and deliverance."

In the same spirit, James wrote, "*Consider it pure joy, my brothers and sisters, whenever you face trials of many kinds, because you know that the testing of your faith produces perseverance...Blessed is the one who perseveres under trial because, having stood the test, that person will receive the crown of life that the Lord has promised to those who love him*" (James 1:2–3, 12).

---

89. Müller, *The Life of Trust*.

3. "With reference to the growth of every grace of the Spirit, it is of the utmost importance that we seek to maintain an upright heart and a good conscience, and, therefore, do not knowingly and habitually indulge in those things which are contrary to the mind of God."

How can believers expect to receive anything from God if they are constantly indulging in sinful actions or thoughts? Nothing saps one's spirit like a guilty conscience. Hidden sin is like a plank in the eye that blocks our view of God.

4. "Let God work for us, when the hour of the trial of our faith comes, and do not work a deliverance of our own."

Too often, believers rush to fix their own problems without allowing time for God to work the best solution. Such an approach only makes matters worse. Faith fails and therefore decreases. Müller wrote that God tries a believer's faith "in order to prove to his child, in the end, how willing he is to help and deliver him, the moment it is good for him."[90]

TWO-STAGE MIRACLES

Two men outside the Bethsaida gate each received a two-stage miracle. Initially, the first-century man healed by Jesus only saw trees walking around. Similarly, I experienced only temporary relief when prayer was offered for my healing. We each received enough to keep trusting in Jesus as the miracle unfolded.

Jesus said all that it takes is a little faith—*"as small as a mustard seed"* (Matthew 17:20)—and one can move mountains. The movement may take a while. The mountain might move in increments. It might seem like nothing is happening, but the mountain *does* move for people of faith.

What about you?

Where do you struggle to believe?

---

90. Ibid.

What would a step of faith look like for you?

What prayer do you need to bring right now to your loving, heavenly Father—for healing, for a restored relationship, or for help in a crisis?

Give it a try.

PRAYER PRINCIPLE #28:

A little faith can move a big mountain.

SECTION FIVE

PRAY ACCORDING TO GOD'S WILL

29

HOW TO KNOW
THE WILL OF GOD

*Do not be conformed to this world, but be transformed by the
renewal of your mind, that by testing you may discern what is the
will of God, what is good and acceptable and perfect.*
—Romans 12:2 (esv)

In 2008, I attended a Narrative Leadership Retreat that focused on
hearing God's voice through the story of one's life. It came at a time when
I was searching for God's will. I had completed a doctorate in Political
Science and wondered about God's journey for me going forward.

Through Scripture reading, storytelling, and other creative elements, I
believe I heard from God that weekend. Strangely, one of the most impact-
ful moments happened when a poem was introduced in one of the sessions.
"The Journey" by Mary Oliver (1935–2019) has since become a kind of
home base for me when I think about vocation:

THE JOURNEY

One day you finally knew
what you had to do, and began,
though the voices around you
kept shouting
their bad advice –
though the whole house
began to tremble
and you felt the old tug
at your ankles.
"Mend my life!"
each voice cried.
But you didn't stop.
You knew what you had to do,
though the wind pried
with its stiff fingers
at the very foundations,
though their melancholy
was terrible.
It was already late
enough, and a wild night,
and the road full of fallen
branches and stones.
But little by little,
as you left their voices behind,
the stars began to burn
through the sheets of clouds,

and there was a new voice

which you slowly

recognized as your own,

that kept you company

as you strode deeper and deeper

into the world,

determined to do

the only thing you could do –

determined to save

the only life you could save.[91]

HEARING FROM GOD

This poem spoke deeply to me. I thought about the voice in my head—the whisper of God—and the way that much of my life was causing me to resist that voice. I felt empowered to take a bold step of faith after that weekend, believing that I better understood God's will for my life.

Each of us is on a journey with God and others. It's a shared journey, but also deeply personal and specific. The truth is that no one knows you like you know you. The deeper truth is that God knows you better than you know you.

> *EACH OF US IS ON A SHARED JOURNEY WITH GOD AND OTHERS, ONE THAT'S DEEPLY PERSONAL AND SPECIFIC. THE TRUTH IS THAT GOD KNOWS YOU BETTER THAN YOU KNOW YOU.*

The journey is not always easy. At times, you may feel like you know what you have to do. At other times, however, you may wonder, *God, how are You leading me? What is Your will?*

91. Mary Oliver, *Dream Work* (New York: The Atlantic Monthly Press, 1986).

God can speak in a thousand ways. God spoke to me through the poem and through other people. God can use animals, nature, newspapers, even television and commercials to get a point across. I heard of a man whose life was changed by a billboard message. I know a woman who read a book that changed the course of her life.

The most reliable, trusted, and available source of hearing God's voice is the Bible. That's why it's called *the Word of God*.

Like a radio frequency, to hear God's voice, you need to be attuned to God's voice. The Word of God helps you do that. It can guide your prayers, make your heart tender, open your eyes to truth, and teach you about God's character. God's Word, along with a humble heart and teachable spirit, can help you know God's will.

> **THE WORD OF GOD CAN GUIDE YOUR PRAYERS, MAKE YOUR HEART TENDER, OPEN YOUR EYES TO TRUTH, AND TEACH YOU ABOUT GOD'S CHARACTER.**

George Müller's success in work and life came from his capacity to know God's will and then do it.

You and I can do the same. We can know God's plans for us, which are always better than our plans for ourselves.

ASCERTAINING GOD'S WILL

Müller laid out five steps for ascertaining God's will.[92]

1. First, Müller said, "I seek at the beginning to get my heart into such a state that it has no will of its own in regard to a given matter. Nine-tenths of the trouble with people generally is at this point. Nine-tenths of the difficulties are overcome when our hearts are ready to do the Lord's will, whatever it may be. When one is truly in this state, it is usually but a little way before one

---

92. Müller, *Release the Power of Prayer*, 103–104.

discovers the knowledge of what God's will is."

Whether you and I know it or not, we often bring before the Lord not only a request for guidance but also an idea about what we think the outcome should be. Seeking God's will first involves emptying ourselves of our own will.

2. Second, Müller wrote, "Having done this, I do not leave the result to feeling or simple impression. If so, I make myself liable to great delusions."

There's nothing wrong with impressions, feelings, or other emotions. Our hearts matter as much as our heads. However, Müller advised keeping emotions in their proper place. We all know how easily we can be misled or mistaken about God's best plans for our lives.

3. Third, Müller wrote, "I seek the will of the Spirit of God through, or in connection with, the Word of God. The Spirit and the Word must be combined. If I look to the Spirit alone without the Word, I also lay myself open to great delusions. If the Holy Spirit guides us at all, He will do it according to the Scriptures and never contrary to them."

It was widely known that Müller read the Bible all the way through four times a year. He grounded every decision in God's Word.

My wife Jen and I have been reading the Moravian Daily Texts for many years. This reading plan guides us through the Bible every two years. We have found that spending time in God's Word provides a strong foundation for making good decisions as individuals and as a couple.

4. Fourth, Müller noted that he took into account "providential circumstances." Looking to see how God was at work in his life, he watched for signs of God's leadership and sought to follow them. "These often plainly indicate God's will in connection with His Word and Spirit."

Our circumstances can be random, but they can also provide a kind of sacred echo. In these moments, there is a certain rhythm as the teachings of Scripture, the impressions given in prayer, and the workings of day-to-day life all combine to suggest where God wants us to go.

THERE IS A CERTAIN RHYTHM AS THE TEACHINGS OF SCRIPTURE, THE IMPRESSIONS GIVEN IN PRAYER, AND THE WORKINGS OF DAY-TO-DAY LIFE ALL COMBINE TO SUGGEST GOD'S WILL.

5. Fifth, Müller wrote, "I ask God in prayer to reveal His will to me so that I may understand it correctly."

That's a bold prayer. And yet should we not expect God, who wants us to do His will, to reveal it? I had a professor who often said, "God doesn't play 'hide the ball' with us. God will show us what God wants us to do if we listen and are willing to obey."

Müller wrote:

Thus, through prayer to God, the study of the Word, and reflection, I come to a deliberate judgment according to the best of my ability and knowledge, and if my mind is thus at peace, and continues to be after two or three more petitions, I proceed accordingly. Both in trivial matters and in transactions involving most important issues, I have found this method always effective.[93]

Note that Müller continued to pray even when he believed that he had heard God's voice. He moved forward deliberately, applying this approach to both small and big decisions.

How often did he find this method effective?

Always.

Have you ever considered that there could be a deliberate, Scripture-centered, proven process for determining God's will for your life?

GOD WANTS TO GUIDE YOU

You aren't alone in your decisions. God wants to guide you and waits for you to approach Him. With the next decision you need to make, try to implement such a process. If you're not reading the Bible every day, begin

---

93. Ibid., 104.

there. Practice emptying yourself of your plans, your expected outcomes, and your ego.

Let God renew your mind. Then you'll know what to do—*"what is good and acceptable and perfect"* (Romans 12:2 ESV).

After the Narrative Leadership Retreat, I began to take practical steps to follow God's will. I can say confidently that it has been an amazing journey although there have been many unexpected turns and strange directions. It was not what I thought it would be, but I believe it has been the best thing that could have happened to me. I'm grateful for the journey.

God has an amazing journey for your life, too. It's the best journey you can take. Will you trust God to lead? You can do many things, but what is the thing that you know you need to do?

Pray now that God would guide your steps and help you to know what you *must* do.

PRAYER PRINCIPLE #29:

God's plans for you are always better than your plans for you.

30

CALL AND RESPONSE

Call to me and I will answer you and tell you great and unsearch-able things you do not know.
—Jeremiah 33:3

Dallas Willard wrote a wonderful book called *Hearing God*. The book challenges followers of Jesus to actually believe that they can expect to hear from God. According to Willard, God is always speaking. The problem is that we don't listen well and don't trust God in all our circumstances.

Willard tells the story of a man named Robert C. McFarlane, who was a well-known businessman in the Los Angeles area. Robert moved to California from Oklahoma in 1970. Within a few days of his arrival—due to an unfortunate misunderstanding with a close friend—he had to assume control of an insurance agency because he had invested a lot of money into it.

After three years, Robert was constantly stressed, tired, and over-whelmed by constant challenges. He also believed that in spite of his experience, he lacked the wisdom to help the company grow.

The silver lining was that McFarlane became a Christian during his time in Los Angeles. His wife and friends had been praying for years for him to make that decision.

One day, after many dark nights of worry and difficult days of exasperation, Robert felt defeated. His financial difficulties closed in on him like a thick fog. While driving to the office, he suddenly felt the urge to turn left onto a road out of town. He wanted to disappear.

HEARING FROM GOD

Then Robert heard a still, small voice piercing his inner turmoil: "Pull over to the curb." He said it was as if the words were written on the windshield. After he pulled over, he heard a different message, as clearly as if someone were in the car with him: "My Son had strains that you will never know, and when he had those strains he turned to me, and that's what you should do."

Robert sat there and wept for a long time. He then drove to the office. When he arrived, twenty-two major problems were waiting for him. However, with God's help and peace, they were substantially resolved by the end of that day.[94]

Robert experienced a spiritual breakthrough that day. I can relate to him in that I have also experienced times when I didn't know what to do next. I have felt the gripping vice of anxiety, the darkness of depression, and the futility of working and working but seeing no results. In those moments, God has spoken to me, too. The message has been the same: *Call to Me. Trust Me. I am with you. I want to help.*

GOD ENCOURAGED THE PROPHET JEREMIAH TO SEEK HIM THROUGH PRAYER AND PROMISED TO ANSWER.

---

94. Dallas Willard, *Hearing God* (Downers Grove, IL: InterVarsity Press, 2012), 28–29.

God instructed Jeremiah, *"Call to me."* These words were spoken not to the Hebrew people generally, but to the prophet himself, encouraging Jeremiah to seek the Lord through prayer. God promised to answer Jeremiah. It's as if God looked down on Jeremiah and said, "Why don't you call on Me?"

What's interesting is that this verse comes in chapter 33 of the book of Jeremiah. The first chapter begins with God telling the prophet that before he was formed in the womb, God knew him and set him apart for service. (See verse 5.) Jeremiah responded, *"I do not know how to speak; I am too young"* (Jeremiah 1:6). However, God replied:

> Do not say, "I am too young." You must go to everyone I send you to and say whatever I command you. Do not be afraid of them, for I am with you and will rescue you.   (Jeremiah 1:7–8)

After this, Jeremiah spoke the Word of God for thirty-two chapters in conversation with God. Nevertheless, in chapter 33, God said, *"Call to me and I will answer."*

The same God who knew Jeremiah in the womb called to him when he was old. When Jeremiah called to Him, God was ready to answer his prayer and share *"unsearchable things"* with him.

Perhaps Jeremiah had forgotten to call to God. Perhaps he had forgotten the help of heaven.

Perhaps we're a lot like Jeremiah.

MÜLLER EXPERIENCES A FLOW OF JOY

After his conversion, George Müller never seemed to forget how to cry out to the living God. One day, when funds were low and nearly one hundred children in his care needed to be fed, Müller called out to God, who answered.

On the evening of July 22, 1838, Müller was walking in his garden, meditating on Hebrews 13:8 (KJV): *"Jesus Christ the same yesterday, and to day, and for ever."* He wrote:

Whilst meditating on his unchangeable love, power, and wisdom… all at once the present need of the Orphan Houses was brought to my mind. Immediately I was led to say to myself, Jesus in his love and power has hitherto supplied me with what I have needed for the orphans, and in the same unchangeable love and power he will provide me with what I may need for the future. A flow of joy came into my soul whilst realizing the unchangeableness of our adorable Lord. About one minute after I had this thought, a letter was brought to me, enclosing a bill for twenty pounds.[95]

The money was enough for the day and then some. What's remarkable is that it was sent *four days before Müller asked for help.*

Through another prophet, God said, *"Before they call I will answer; while they are still speaking I will hear"* (Isaiah 65:24).

MOST PEOPLE DON'T HAVE DIFFICULTY PRAYING SIMPLE PRAYERS. BUT TO BRING A SPECIFIC NEED BEFORE GOD IN EXTENDED AND QUIET PRAYER IS ANOTHER THING ENTIRELY.

Most people don't have difficulty praying simple prayers. Lots of people pray in the morning; some pray throughout the day. To really call out to God—to bring a specific need before God in extended and quiet prayer is another thing entirely. To call out to God in simple trust and expect an answer is next-level faith.

Would God look at you and say, "You talk to Me. You pray to Me. But you don't really call out to Me in the belief that I have everything you need"?

When we pray according to God's will, we can expect answers. Müller prayed that God would supply the basic needs of the children under his roof. He trusted that God would supply the needs, not because Müller was

---

95. Müller, *The Life of Trust.*

deserving or worthy of such gifts, but because Müller believed that everything depended on the living God's merits and worth.

Do you seek God's face for what you want and need?

Some people need healing from a past pain. Some people need freedom from a bad habit. Some people find their minds overwhelmed with anxiety. Some people need physical healing.

God is waiting for you. Why delay in calling on Him?

We must not only seek God and wait upon Him for deliverance but also remember that God waits upon us and seeks us out.

> The LORD waits to be gracious to you, and therefore he exalts himself to show mercy to you. For the LORD is a God of justice; blessed are all those who wait for him. (Isaiah 30:18 ESV)

Maybe there is doubt in your heart that God really cares. Tell God about your doubt and ask Him to increase your faith. Maybe you're tired after praying for so long for the same thing. Tell God that you're weary and ask Him to help you pray. Ask the Holy Spirit to well up prayer and faith within you.

WRITE DOWN PRAYER REQUESTS

One new spiritual practice I have undertaken by studying George Müller's life is to write down prayer requests. I have often done spiritual journaling in the past, but now I specifically keep a record of those prayers. I go back and review the record sometimes, making a check mark beside answered prayer. I'm amazed by how many check marks I'm making.

The same God who said to Jeremiah, *"Call to me"* is the One who speaks to you today.

When you call to God, He will answer and tell you *"unsearchable things"* you do not know. These are things that are inaccessible to us, secret things, and mighty things. What an amazing promise that God's whisper will reach your ears to share truth and understanding. In relationships, you will receive wisdom to navigate what seems impossible to overcome. God will tell you information about your future, promises that will be fulfilled, and dreams that He wants to walk out in your life.

You won't know these things unless you pray.

When Jesus was under pressure—even led to the cross and nailed to the beams—He turned to God for help. You should do the same.

Pray now. Call to God. Expect that God will answer.

PRAYER PRINCIPLE #30:

God waits to tell you unsearchable things and give you the help of heaven.

31

GOD'S DREAM TEAM

Again, truly I tell you that if two of you on earth agree about any-
thing they ask for, it will be done for them by my Father in heaven.
For where two or three gather in my name, there am I with them.
—Matthew 18:19–20

In 1992, the world was captivated by a group called the Dream Team. It was the first year that professional basketball players were allowed to play in the Olympics. Typically, only amateurs were allowed to compete; but that year, Team USA stacked the court with National Basketball League (NBA) players like the Chicago Bulls' Michael Jordan and Scottie Pippin, the Boston Celtics' Larry Bird, the New York Knicks' Patrick Ewing, and the Philadelphia 76ers' Charles Barclay.

The team was described as the greatest sports team ever assembled. On their way to the gold, the Dream Team beat every other team by an average of 44 points. Germany, Angola, Brazil—no one could even come close to challenging them. More than that, they were obviously having a blast playing together.

However, many people don't know that they actually lost one game. In June before the Olympics, Coach Chuck Daly organized a scrimmage of college players against the Dream Team. The pros looked like a mess—out of sync, missing shots, giving up rebounds—while the college students dominated.[96]

THE IMPORTANCE OF TEAMWORK

Coach Daly knew what the problem was immediately. In spite of all the talent on the court, the players needed to let go of their egos. They needed to forget their respective NBA teams and focus on being one team, Team USA.

When you're working on the same team, it doesn't matter what you look like, where you come from, or how you view the world. It doesn't matter what tribe or class or culture you call home. As long as the person working beside you shares your goals and knows the importance of working together, you can accomplish your task.

> *GOD HAS PLACED YOU ON A TEAM WITH PEOPLE WHO HAVE DIFFERENT GIFTS AND TALENTS. YOUR GOAL IS TO SEE GOD GET THE GLORY AND SHARE THE GOOD NEWS WITH THE WORLD.*

God has a mission for the church of making disciples. To accomplish that goal, God places you on a team with people who have different gifts and talents. The common goal is to see God get the glory and share the good news with the whole world. God's dream is to see not only a growing family of forgiven, grace-filled brothers and sisters but also a united church working well together in the Holy Spirit's power.

The problem is that we often fail to play as a team. We don't value all gifts the same. We don't care for the poor as much as we comfort the wealthy.

---

96. Kevin Moore, "The 1 Game That the Dream Team Lost Did Not Happen During the Olympics," April 27, 2020, accessed August 25, 2021, www.sportscasting.com/the-one-game-that-the-dream-team-lost-did-not-happen-during-the-olympics.

PRAYING WITH OTHERS

Maybe worst of all, we don't pray for one another. We don't pray *with* one another.

The Bible is clear about the importance of working together in prayer. James wrote:

> *Is anyone among you sick? Let him call for the elders of the church, and let them pray over him, anointing him with oil in the name of the Lord. And the prayer of faith will save the one who is sick, and the Lord will raise him up.* (James 5:14–15 ESV)

Paul wrote to his protégé Timothy, "*First of all, then, I urge that supplications, prayers, intercessions, and thanksgivings be made for all people*" (1 Timothy 2:1 ESV).

Scripture is clear. We're called to work together as a team, including the work of prayer.

In July 1835, a man George Müller called "brother C——r" joined him in the work of serving parishioners in Bristol, England. He helped Müller for two years. They prayed often and "unitedly, chiefly about the schools and the circulation of the Scriptures" and "repeatedly together respecting the funds."[97]

In one of the most difficult times of trial, Müller recorded what can happen when God's people pray together. On Monday, September 10, 1838, he wrote:

> Neither Saturday nor yesterday had any money come in. It appeared to me now needful to take some steps on account of our need, i.e., to go to the Orphan Houses, call the brethren and sisters together...state the case to them, see how much money was needed for the present, tell them that amidst all this trial of faith I still believed that God would help, and to pray with them.[98]

---

97. Müller, *The Life of Trust*.
98. Ibid.

In Müller's mind, a solemn crisis had come over the orphanages. A small amount of money was given soon after their prayer, but much more was needed. Müller wrote:

> About ten, after I had returned from brother Craik, to whom I had unbosomed my heart again, whilst once more in prayer for help, a sister called who gave two sovereigns to my wife for the orphans, stating that she had felt herself stirred up to come, and that she had delayed coming already too long. A few minutes after, when I went into the room where she was, she gave me two sovereigns more, and all this without knowing the least about our need. Thus the Lord most mercifully has sent us a little help, to the great encouragement of my faith.[99]

Notice that Müller's first instinct was not only to pray but also to gather others to pray with him.

WHEN THE HOLY SPIRIT FELL ON THE DAY OF PENTECOST, THOUSANDS OF BELIEVERS BECAME PART OF GOD'S MISSION.

When the Holy Spirit fell on the day of Pentecost, three thousand people were baptized. These believers began to meet together for fellowship, to teach, and to share what they had with those in need. They were now part of God's mission, part of God's *dream team*. They no longer lived for themselves. They had a new leader in Jesus Christ—a new coach to guide their lives.

Therefore, it was only a matter of time before they ran into trouble. Peter and John were walking into the temple one day when they saw a crippled man, who asked them for money. Peter responded, *"Silver or gold I do not have, but what I do have I give you. In the name of Jesus Christ of Nazareth, walk"* (Acts 3:6). Feeling strength in his legs, the man stood up and started leaping and praising God.

---

99. Ibid.

OPPOSITION TO MIRACLES

You might think everyone would have been happy about that miracle, but afterward, Peter and John faced fierce opposition. They were thrown into jail and forbidden to speak about Jesus anymore. However, the two apostles said, *"Which is right in God's eyes: to listen to you, or to him? You be the judges! As for us, we cannot help speaking about what we have seen and heard"* (Acts 4:19–20).

More and more lives were being changed by the gospel, but at the same time, the threats against the early church grew. There were people like Saul, who hated believers and sought to destroy the church. (See Acts 8:3.)

This did not deter Peter, John, and the rest of Jesus's followers in the least. After the chief priests and Jewish elders released them, they gathered together and prayed as a group. They prayed:

> *Sovereign Lord…you made the heavens and the earth and the sea, and everything in them. You spoke by the Holy Spirit through the mouth of your servant, our father David: "Why do the nations rage and the peoples plot in vain? The kings of the earth rise up and the rulers band together against the Lord and against his anointed one."…Now, Lord, consider their threats and enable your servants to speak your word with great boldness.* (Acts 4:24–26, 29)

When they had prayed, the Holy Spirit shook the place where they were meeting. They then went out filled with power and preached the Word of God with boldness. (See verse 31.)

When life starts to shake—through grief, loss, uncertainty, disappointment, or defeat—God's people need to start praying. When the early church prayed, they were filled with a fresh power.

JESUS GAVE US A PHENOMENAL PROMISE: IF TWO BELIEVERS AGREE AND BRING ANY NEED BEFORE GOD IN PRAYER, HE WILL ANSWER.

Jesus gave us a phenomenal promise: if two believers agree and bring any need before God in prayer, He will answer. It may not be at the same time or the same way that they want, but *"it will be done for them by my Father in heaven"* (Matthew 18:19).

Have you been playing alone when God wants you to play with a team?

Have you expressed your heart's great needs to others so they can pray with you, or has your ego stood in the way?

Reach out to a friend or family member today. Ask them to pray for you or with you. God may be waiting for you to pray with others before He answers your prayer.

You're not alone. You're on God's dream team. Do your part to pray a better world into being.

PRAYER PRINCIPLE #31:

When it comes to prayer, two or three are better than one.

32

GET OFF THE MAP

And we all, who with unveiled faces contemplate the Lord's glory,
are being transformed into his image with ever-increasing glory,
which comes from the Lord, who is the Spirit.
—2 Corinthians 3:18

Y ou never know how one conversation can change someone's life. When I was a junior in college, I had one of those conversations.

Although I was following Christ, I had been living with one foot in, one foot out. The walk did not match the talk. I was struggling.

The Baptist Student Union (BSU) on campus had a minister named Dick Ferrell, who was always up for a conversation over a game of ping-pong. So I made my way over to the BSU for a game and a talk. Dick and I discussed purpose, how to hear God's voice, and how to discern God's will. Back and forth, back and forth. I had a lot of questions. I was ashamed of the way I had been living. Although I don't remember exactly what Dick said, I know that it altered my life. I started not only changing some of my life patterns but also planning for seminary.

One conversation can change a life.

LIFE-CHANGING CONVERSATIONS

The Bible is full of life-changing conversations. On the road to Damascus, Saul saw a blinding light and heard a voice saying, *"Saul, Saul, why do you persecute me?"* (Acts 9:4). As a result of his conversation with Jesus, Saul was forever changed.

A conversation with Jesus changed the life of a woman He met at a well. He said to her, *"If you knew the gift of God and who it is that asks you for a drink, you would have asked him and he would have given you living water"* (John 4:10). She left her water jar and went running off to tell other people about Jesus.

A conversation by the seashore transformed four fishermen into a world-changing movement. *"'Come, follow me,' Jesus said, 'and I will send you out to fish for people'"* (Matthew 4:19).

Sometimes we are afraid to pray because we know some of the things God says. To say "Jesus is Lord" means that He's Lord of everything or nothing at all.

In prayer, God deals with our will, our wants, our hurts, and our hang-ups so that we'll be conformed to the image of Christ. As His Word tells us:

> And we all, who with unveiled faces contemplate the Lord's glory, are being transformed into his image with ever-increasing glory, which comes from the Lord, who is the Spirit.   (2 Corinthians 3:18)

God invites us to communicate with Him with *"unveiled faces."* This image reminds us of Moses, who had a special relationship with God and spoke to Him like a friend. (See Exodus 33:11.) After Moses spoke to God face to face on Mount Sinai, his face was glowing so radiantly that he had to cover it with a veil in the presence of the Israelites because *"they were afraid to come near him"* (Exodus 34:30).

A FRIEND OF SINNERS

Jesus referred to His disciples as His friends. (See John 15:15.) He was a friend of sinners. (See Matthew 11:19.) Because of His sacrifice on the cross, we can be restored into a right relationship with God. The *veil* of both sin and fear before God has been removed. We can now approach God unveiled, and talk to Him as a friend, face to face.

> **WE ARE INVITED INTO AN HONEST, INTIMATE CONVERSATION WITH GOD, TALKING TO HIM AS A FRIEND, FACE TO FACE.**

Think of what this means. No more pretense. No more hiding. We are invited into an honest, intimate conversation with God. Whether our prayers are silent, spoken, mystical, or congregational, all prayers are about intimate conversation with God.

Do you talk to God as a friend with an unveiled face?

THE SKEPTIC AND THE BARON

George Müller related the story of a young man named Thomas and a wealthy Prussian businessman, Baron von Kamp. The baron helped seminary students. Thomas heard about the baron's generosity and wrote to ask for support.

At that time, priestly positions were very lucrative, so much so that even people with little or no faith went into ministry. That was the case of the young man. Despite planning to serve in the ministry, he was argumentative and showed contempt for the Bible and the gospel.

Taking an interest in him, the baron invited Thomas to stay in his home. While the baron took pains to serve him every evening, the young man kept challenging the baron's beliefs. Never debating him, the baron just continued to help Thomas in practical ways, such as helping him remove his boots, and speaking kindly to him.

One evening, Thomas became exasperated by the way the baron served him in such menial ways. He cried, "Baron, how can you do all this? You see I do not care about you. How are you able to continue to be so kind to me and serve me like this?" The baron replied, "My dear young friend,

I have learned it from the Lord Jesus. I wish you would read through the Gospel of John. Good night."

Thomas was so moved that he sat down to read the Word of God with an open heart and a willingness to learn. It pleased God to bless him, and he became a follower of Jesus Christ.[100]

The young man was changed by an earthly conversation that morphed into a divine conversation.

What keeps you from intimate, unveiled conversation with your heavenly Father? Can you see the possibilities you are missing because you refuse to persist in prayer?

It's sad when children only want to talk to their parents about what they want or need. The parent/child relationship is developed only by conversation that delves into deeper things—beliefs, emotions, desires, and honest dialogue about any issues that may be driving them apart.

> **EVEN THOUGH GOD KNOWS WHAT YOU WANT AND NEED BEFORE YOU ASK, HE IS PLEASED WHEN YOU COME TO HIM IN A POSTURE OF GRATEFULNESS.**

Even though God knows what you want and need before you ask, He is pleased when you come to Him in a posture of gratefulness, glorifying Him for His consistent presence in your life. God wants to be close to you so that you can be satisfied not only externally, but on the soul level. You were designed for divine conversations.

HOW TO PRAY MORE INTIMATELY

Here are two principles that can help you pray more intimately.

---

100. Müller, "Encouragement to Those with Unconverted Family and Friends," www. georgemuller.org/devotional/encouragement-to-those-with-unconverted-family-and-friends1885762.

First, talk less. Don't fill up the air with many words. (See Matthew 6:7.) We are invited to come before God with unveiled faces to contemplate or behold His glory. Prayer is both contemplating and communicating. Prayer is beholding and becoming.

Take time each day just to sit in the Lord's presence. I have found it helpful to have a few minutes of silence before reading Scripture and praying. It centers my heart and allows me to empty myself of my motives and expectations.

Second, listen more. How will you hear God if there's only room for what you say to Him? People rarely wait in prayer because they don't expect to be answered in prayer. Thus, they fill the space with phrases that generally sound the same to God's ears.

God says, "*Call to me and I will answer you, and will tell you great and hidden things that you have not known*" (Jeremiah 33:3 ESV). God may answer you in prayer. He may tell you *"great and hidden things"* only after you repeatedly pray for many days. God can also answer you as you listen to others and discern God's voice through your circumstances.

GETTING OFF THE MAP

The motivational speaker Bob Goff was teaching at Pepperdine University when a senior student named John took his class. John and a few friends wanted to serve Christ after graduation, but they didn't know what to do. They invited Bob to their home. As they sat around the fire pit, they told Bob that they didn't want to lead typical lives, they wanted to do something to get "off the map." Bob looked at John and said, "I dare you to spin the globe, throw your finger down, and pick a place to plug in. And if you don't have any other place you'd rather go, why not Uganda?" Bob had been working in Uganda for five years. Within a few weeks, Bob and John boarded a plane to Kampala, Uganda.

Uganda had been ravaged by a long civil war. Tens of thousands of children had been abducted by militant groups and forced to fight with machine guns. Against their will, young girls became child brides. After the war, thousands of children were living in government camps and receiving no education.

Bob and John overcome all kinds of barriers to start a school called Restore Leadership Academy. When Bob flew home, John's task was to put together the best teachers and recruit the best students. Soon they had a hundred kids and an amazing group of adults to care for them.

John called Bob one night to tell him about the school's success and about two kids who were walking eight miles a day to attend classes. He asked, "Bob, would it be possible to give these two kids a place to stay overnight?" Bob responded, "Absolutely not! We're not a boarding school."

John persisted, "But Bob, this is what these kids need. We just need two bunks. That's all, two bunks."

Bob responded, "No, John."

"But it's for the kids," John still persisted.

Finally, Bob relented. "Alright John, two bunks. That's all, no more."

As of 2017, over two hundred and fifty students were boarding at Restore Leadership Academy. And John has been affectionately nicknamed Two-Bunk John.[101]

It all happened because he had a conversation that changed his life as well as the lives of hundreds of children. It led to a deeper, amazing adventure of following Jesus.

If one human conversation can change a life, think of what one conversation with God can do.

Believe that God speaks. Believe that God will give you wisdom when you ask for it. Believe that God does not want you to live a mundane life, but a great adventure. Let your belief inform the way you pray. Stop praying as usual. "Get off the map" and explore a richer, more rewarding way to pray in your heavenly Father's presence.

God calls you *friend*. Why don't you speak to your friend right now?

PRAYER PRINCIPLE #32:

You were designed for divine communication.

---

101. Bob Goff, *Love Does* (Nashville, TN: Thomas Nelson, 2012), 206–212.

33

LIFE'S FIRST AND GREATEST CONCERN

Seek first his kingdom and his righteousness, and all these things
will be given to you as well.
—Matthew 6:33

When my daughter Emily was two years old, I buckled her in the car for what I thought would be a fun adventure. She had never been through an automatic car wash—the kind where you put the car in neutral as the machine guides it through soaping, brushing, and rinsing.

I watched her in the rearview mirror as we moved ahead. At first, her eyes were wide with wonder, but soon, she began to look worried and then panic-stricken. Finally, she burst into tears. She was terrified.

"Emily, don't be afraid," I said. "We're safe. It's almost over."

She calmed down, but I know that she was glad when we exited the car wash. I was glad too. Who wants their child to be filled with anxiety and fear?

THE AGE OF ANXIETY

God doesn't want *us* to be worried and fearful either, but it's really hard to avoid such feelings these days. We live in a time that's been called *the age of anxiety*. We're worried about the future. We're worried about our country. We're worried about what the church will be like in the coming years. We're worried that worry consumes us.

Worry is constant. Imagine a single mom lying awake at 2 a.m. She can't sleep because her mind can't let go of her daily responsibilities of raising children, keeping up with schoolwork, doing housework, and somehow holding onto her job. Imagine the small business owner struggling to rebound from a hard economic year under the shadow of COVID-19. Imagine the senior adult who can't keep pace with changing technology and is alone many days without a satisfying connection to others.

> **AS MUCH AS WE MAY THINK OF THE NEEDS OF OTHERS, WE MOSTLY WORRY ABOUT OURSELVES.**

As much as we may think of the needs of others, we can't help but think about our own future. We mostly worry about ourselves—our busy plans, changes at work or school, or our health or finances. We are afraid of the anger we see in our country. We feel somehow responsible or at least complacent. We feel helpless.

God knows we worry.

But let's look at the good news. According to Matthew 9:36, "*When* [Jesus] *saw the crowds, he had compassion on them, because they were harassed and helpless, like sheep without a shepherd.*"

JESUS BRINGS PEACE

Jesus wasn't like other religious leaders who were always at the temple, never mixing with the common people. He was always in the middle of it all. He was compassionate and available for interactions in the streets.

He went to the sickbeds. He walked for miles to reach people like the Samaritan woman at a well. He saw the people and knew they were harassed and helpless. His presence gave hope, and something about Him brought peace. Wherever He went, things got better.

Has it ever struck you how happy and calm Jesus was? We know that He was *"a man of sorrows and acquainted with grief"* (Isaiah 53:3 ESV). We know that He went through darkness and suffered the worst kind of humiliation and death on a cross. We know He wept at the tomb of His friend Lazarus. We know that zeal for His Father's house led him to overturn the money changers' tables at the temple.

These are exceptions, however, to the deep peace and confidence with which Jesus lived despite the trouble all around Him. Watching the birds, He noticed that although they never seemed to work or worry like people do, they were provided for. He said, *"Look at the birds of the air; they do not sow or reap or store away in barns, and yet your heavenly Father feeds them"* (Matthew 6:26).

Jesus had seen thousands of flowers and knew they could be gone tomorrow, consumed by fire, trampled by an animal, or wilting for lack of rain. They didn't spend time putting on makeup or shopping for new clothes, but they were beautiful in and of themselves. They were so different from people who were worried and anxious all the time, running around after things, concerned about what they had or didn't have. (See verses 28–31.)

> **JESUS'S COMPASSION WAS SO GREAT THAT HE WANTED PEOPLE TO KNOW THE FIRST PRINCIPLE TO LIVING WITH PEACE: SEEKING GOD'S KINGDOM FIRST.**

Jesus's compassion was so great that He wanted people to know the first principle to living with peace: *"Seek the Kingdom of God above all else, and live righteously, and he will give you everything you need"* (Matthew 6:33 NLT). That was an extraordinary teaching. We argue the exact opposite: "Well, I *must* live, I *must* make a certain amount of money, I *must* be clothed, I *must* be fed." The great concerns of our lives are not about God's kingdom but how we will care for ourselves.

Jesus taught us a better way, His way. We must get our relationship right with God first, pursuing His kingdom and His righteousness, and looking to others' needs. Then He will give us everything else.

QUESTIONS THAT STIR THE SOUL

George Müller referenced Matthew 6:33 in speaking of the need to pray for external prosperity so that God's kingdom would advance and people would turn their souls toward Christ. He also said people must pray for internal prosperity so that God's children can have the resources they need.

Then he posed some challenging questions. When I first read them, they stirred my soul and caused some conviction. Müller wrote:

> I now ask you, my dear reader, a few questions in all love, because I do seek your welfare, and I do not wish to put these questions to you without putting them first to my own heart. Do you make it your primary business, your first great concern, to seek the kingdom of God and his righteousness? Are the things of God, the honor of his name, the welfare of his church, the conversion of sinners, and the profit of your own soul, your chief aim? Or does your business, or your family, or your own temporal concerns, in some shape or other primarily occupy your attention?[102]

Referring to Jesus's words about seeking the kingdom first, Müller stated, "I never knew a child of God, who acted according to the above passage, in whose experience the Lord did not fulfil his word of promise, *'All these things shall be added unto you.'"*[103]

Seeking God's kingdom and God's righteousness *first* is not just a nice saying. It is a strategy that leads to peace.

---

102. Müller, *The Life of Trust.*
103. Ibid.

When you pray, do your prayers focus on God's kingdom, God's way, and God's provision for others, or are they mostly concerned with your kingdom, your way, and your provisions?

If you have been living for your own way and prosperity, then ask God to forgive you and to help you apply Jesus's teaching to your life.

Seeking God's kingdom *first* means finding out what matters most and building your life around it. Each day, we face distractions and competition for our attention. Pushing back against a me-first, consumeristic system can feel almost impossible. But Jesus said that only one thing can change everything: "Seek *first* the kingdom of God."

THE KINGDOM IS A VISION OF GOD'S LOVING REIGN TO RECONCILE EVERYONE AND EVERYTHING TO GOD AND RENEW CREATION.

The kingdom is a vision of God's loving reign to reconcile everyone and everything to God and renew creation, even the systems that are unjust. It is God's manifest peace.

The problem is that we spend most of our lives trying to build our own kingdoms.

Have you ever seen a child building a sandcastle on the beach near the water's edge? She does all she can to protect it against the waves coming in. That's a picture of modern American life. Jesus says the point of life is not found in money or things. God knows you need them, but first seek His presence to please Him. Seek to spread His way of forgiveness, to welcome strangers, little ones, and the elderly, and to give generously from what you have been given.

Seek first God's righteousness. The word *righteousness* means God's right ways, His holiness in your mind and body. God desires that you have a holy, set-apart life. The word *righteousness* can also be translated *justice.* Seek fairness and equity—righteous deeds on behalf of others. God is urging us to choose compassion and justice that manifest His kingdom in the middle of the trouble we encounter in our world.

WHAT GOD WANTS MOST

We may think, *God wants me to be a good person, to show up for worship, and to give my money.* These things are important. However, through the prophet Amos, we learn that what God wants most is justice and right living, not religious ceremonies. *"Let justice run down like water, and righteousness like a mighty stream"* (Amos 5:24 NKJV). If we simply "do church" and ignore the injustice in our society, it is too weak to say that we disappoint God. Amos says that God despises such a church. (See Amos 5:21–23.)

Jesus walked into the middle of humanity's tragedy and offered a revolutionary teaching. When you seek God's kingdom and His righteousness, *"all these things will be given to you as well"* (Matthew 6:33). God knows you need things to live. Those things matter. If you seek God's kingdom, however, and work so that others will have what they need, you won't have to worry about your life. You'll be living justly, trusting in God to take care of you.

You'll have peace.

Today, ask God to help you reorient your prayers. Ask God to help you to know what it means to seek His kingdom and righteousness. Ask God to give you courage to live differently.

Can you imagine what the world would be like if we all did this? Can you imagine every child's stomach full? Can you envision every child having a great education? Can you see every person living into old age, honored and cared for, with every person receiving justice equally, no matter the color of their skin? Can you imagine the anxiety of our age dissipating, with every man and woman and child at peace?

Jesus said, *"In this world you will have trouble. But take heart! I have overcome the world"* (John 16:33). He has shown us the way to peace: *"Peace I leave with you; my peace I give you. I do not give to you as the world gives. Do not let your hearts be troubled and do not be afraid"* (John 14:27).

PRAYER PRINCIPLE #33:

When you pray first for God's kingdom, everything else falls into place.

34

THE FIERY TRIAL

Thy will be done.
—Matthew 6:10 (KJV)

My wife Jen was driving on the interstate when one of the tires on her car suddenly exploded. The tire not only burst, shredding and slinging rubber everywhere, but it also damaged the wheel well, shattered the headlight, and left a trail of metal and plastic as the debris pinballed under her car. The estimate for the mechanical and body repairs was over $5,000. Our insurance company refused to pay for the repairs, saying that Jen didn't have an accident. They said it was an act of God.

I plan to ask God about that when I get to heaven.

The repairs took many weeks. In the meantime, Jen rented a car. On her way to pick up the repaired car, Jen was driving the rental car on the interstate. Without warning, it started to act strangely. As the dashboard went haywire, Jen smelled smoke coming through the air conditioning vents. Then she saw flames springing from the hood. Pulling over quickly, she tried to get out, but the power locks didn't work because the electrical system was malfunctioning. Finally forcing the door open, she narrowly escaped as the car burned to the ground.

An act of God was starting to sound believable. We gave thanks that she was okay, but both events shook her up.

TROUBLES WILL COME

Every person faces troubles. We call these circumstances by different names—difficulties, trials, tribulations, afflictions—but they come to all of us. Most people do their best to avoid trouble, but trouble has a way of finding us anyway.

Jesus said, *"In this world you will have trouble"* (John 16:33).

So true. Financial trouble. Medical trouble. Marriage trouble. Career trouble.

> **SOMETIMES WE GET OURSELVES INTO TROUBLE. WE SIN OR STRAY. IN THOSE TIMES, WE CAN EXPECT OUR HEAVENLY FATHER TO CHASTISE US.**

Sometimes we get ourselves into trouble. We sin or stray. In those times, as God's children, we can expect our heavenly Father to chastise us by sending His rod of correction. However, according to Hebrews 12:11, *"No discipline seems pleasant at the time, but painful. Later on, however, it produces a harvest of righteousness and peace for those who have been trained by it."*

Sometimes the devil brings us trouble. God allows temptation to test our commitment to Him or expose our ungodly desires. James 1:14–15 (ESV) says, *"Each person is tempted when he is lured and enticed by his own desire. Then desire when it has conceived gives birth to sin, and sin when it is fully grown brings forth death."*

In these times, God desires for us to turn to Him and receive the strength we need to resist.

> No temptation has overtaken you except what is common to mankind. And God is faithful; he will not let you be tempted beyond what you can bear. But when you are tempted, he will also provide a way out so that you can endure it.   (1 Corinthians 10:13)

Sometimes we face trouble not due to sin or temptation, but because God allows a trial of faith. Trials may be seasons of struggle, hard and unexpected circumstances, or tasks that God places before us. When trials come, we often ask two questions:

1. How am I going to get through this?

2. Does anybody care?

We wonder where we'll find the resources to endure and if anyone sees what we're going through.

"IT PLEASED THE LORD TO TRY MY FAITH"

In July 1853, George Müller wrote, "It pleased the Lord to try my faith in a way in which before it had not been tried. My beloved daughter, an only child, and a believer since the commencement of the year 1846, was taken ill on June 20. This illness, at first a low fever, turned to typhus."[104]

God sustained Müller and his wife as they cared for their daughter. As she approached death, Müller didn't give up. He continued in prayer. As a result, a sense of peace came over him. He felt "satisfied with the will of [his] heavenly Father, being assured that he would only do that for her and her parents which in the end would be the best."[105]

He also felt assured regarding the affliction's cause. It was not the rod of correction for any lukewarmness in his or his daughter's soul. He did not feel he was being tempted in his weakened state to turn his back on God. Rather, he said:

---

104. Müller, *The Life of Trust*.
105. Ibid.

The Lord would try my faith concerning one of my dearest earthly treasures, yea, next to my beloved wife, the dearest of all of my earthly possessions. Parents know what an only child, a beloved child, is, and what to believing parents an only child, a believing child, must be…the Father in heaven said…Art thou willing to give up this child to me? My heart responded, As it seems good to thee, my heavenly Father. Thy will be done.[106]

According to Müller, his daughter's illness was his greatest trial of faith. We should not think for a minute that it was easy for him to pray that prayer. Müller was no cold, mechanical believer. He grieved deeply for his daughter's suffering and through faith brought his greatest need to his heavenly Father.

His daughter lived. After her recovery, Müller reflected on one of my favorite verses: *"Delight thyself also in the LORD: and he shall give thee the desires of thine heart"* (Psalm 37:4 KJV). Müller's desire was to keep his beloved daughter, but somehow he was able to delight first in God's will.

I honestly can't say if I would have had the same faith. I don't know if I would have stood up under the trial, willing to give up my children, Christopher or Emily, or to say, *"Thy will be done."*

TRIALS CAN GROW FAITH

How about you? Are you in the fiery trial of faith? Are your circumstances dark? Do you wonder about God's goodness? If so, then offer your trouble, temptation, or trial to God.

First, believe that God is growing faith in you. God is allowing the difficulty to happen for your good.

Count it all joy, my brothers, when you meet trials of various kinds, for you know that the testing of your faith produces steadfastness. And let steadfastness have its full effect, that you may be perfect and complete, lacking in nothing. (James 1:2–4 ESV)

---

106. Ibid.

Second, depend on prayer to see you through. *"Be joyful in hope, patient in affliction, faithful in prayer"* (Romans 12:12).

Third, give thanks and praise in the time of trial. *"These* [trials] *have come so that the proven genuineness of your faith—of greater worth than gold, which perishes even though refined by fire—may result in praise, glory and honor when Jesus Christ is revealed"* (1 Peter 1:7).

Thank God for your blessings. Sing a song, even if you don't feel like it. Trust that God is receiving glory through your trial and that His character is being revealed. Faith is believing that God is good in the midst of bad times, kind in the face of cruel circumstances, loving in the day of evil, and faithful when all else fails.

> **GOD IS GOOD IN THE MIDST OF BAD TIMES, KIND IN THE FACE OF CRUEL CIRCUMSTANCES, LOVING IN THE DAY OF EVIL, AND FAITHFUL WHEN ALL ELSE FAILS.**

In *My Utmost for His Highest*, Oswald Chambers wrote, "Faith by its very nature must be tested and tried. And the real trial of faith is not that we find it difficult to trust God, but that God's character must be proven as trustworthy in our own minds."[107]

Perhaps the greatest turn of the heart happens when we can no longer say, "My will be done," but instead, *"Thy will be done"* (Matthew 6:10 KJV).

If you're not in the fiery trial of faith, don't wait until it happens to pray. Pray now for the trouble or test that is bound to come sooner or later.

The evangelist R. A. Torrey wrote, "Many fail in the battle because they wait until the hour of battle to ask for aid. Others succeed because they have gained victory on their knees long before the battle arrived…

---

107. Oswald Chambers, "The Trial of Faith," *My Utmost for His Highest*, accessed August 25, 2021, utmost.org/the-trial-of-faith.

Anticipate your battles, fight them on your knees before temptation comes, and you will always have victory."[108]

Trouble is going to come. Be ready. Trust God. Pray now.

PRAYER PRINCIPLE #34:

In the trial of faith, trust in God's goodness.

108. R. A. Torrey, *Your Life in God* (New Kensington, PA: Whitaker House, 1984), 77.

SECTION SIX

PERSIST IN PRAYER

35

HOW DOES YOUR
GARDEN GROW?

*Jesus told his disciples a parable to show them that they should
always pray and not give up.*
—Luke 18:1

Some years ago, my wife Jen and I experienced a change in the way we
saw ourselves, our marriage, and our home. For all the years we had been
together, we knew that we wanted God to use our home for His purposes.
We also felt called in our respective vocations—pastoring churches and
nursing. The shift came when we started to see ourselves as *missionaries* to
the people who lived near us.

God began to grow a dual calling in us. In addition to my working for
the church and Jen's serving as a nurse, we also sought to bless our neighbors and do all we could to help them know Jesus. We started to move
toward one unified calling that would transcend our roles in the community. The calling was to live for Christ and bring glory to God whether we
were at home or at work, having fun in the community, going to dinner
with friends, or doing something else. We wanted to live out Colossians

3:17: "*Whatever you do, whether in word or deed, do it all in the name of the Lord Jesus, giving thanks to God the Father through him.*"

Jen and I began to pray for God to reveal how He could use us. We wanted to be in relationship with others.

A LONG-AWAITED HARVEST

Our desire intensified for our home to be available to anyone who needed a friend or family. As we prayed, however, nothing happened.

For five years.

It wasn't that we weren't trying. We hosted dinner parties and outdoor events. These were well-attended, but the relationships stayed on the surface. I began to wonder when we would stop talking about sports, politics, and entertainment and start talking about real things. We had a vision for a growing spiritual family based on faith, not biology. We imagined people coming together to share their possessions and live in deep, authentic relationships while learning the way of Jesus. It would be a family in which everyone was welcome, whether people were just a few steps along or far down the road of faith.

So why wasn't it working?

AFTER FIVE YEARS OF PRAYING AND TRYING, I WANTED TO GIVE UP. THEN I TOOK MY HANDS OFF THE WHEEL AND SIMPLY BEGAN TO PRAY.

After five years of praying and trying, I wanted to give up. I said, "Lord, I can't do this. Everything that I'm trying is failing." I took my hands off the wheel and simply began to pray, "God, do what You want to do. Show me how to love and care for my neighbors. Make this what You want it to be. Or if You'll receive more glory if nothing happens, I can live with that. But I want to see the kingdom come in my neighborhood."

I prayed that prayer for about a month. Then things began to move.

THE GARDEN GROWS

Out of the blue, a neighbor approached me about having a block party. She said she would take care of all the details. All I needed to do was spread the word and show up. Having been connected to our church for a little while, she seemed to have the same vision as ours. Soon after we started making plans, another family from our neighborhood began attending our church. Our three families reached out to invite a few more families. Rather than focusing on the whole neighborhood, we focused on two blocks, consisting of about thirty homes.

The word began to spread about our get-together. We were amazed when over forty people showed up. I met people I had never met before. There was food, energy, and lots of laughter.

People were making connections and forming new relationships. After the event, we were left asking, "What's next?" We decided to host a dinner and talk about forming a local group—an outpost of the kingdom in our neighborhood—with the simple idea of being a blessing to others. Four families came to the dinner. We then decided to meet with that group, along with anyone else who wanted to come, every other week on Sunday evenings.

Our format was simple. We rotated homes, with one home hosting the adult gathering and a second home hosting the kids with childcare. Everyone brought an appetizer to share, although one woman with mad baking skills offered to bring dessert every time. We checked in with each other at every gathering, talked about how each family was doing, and prayed for one another. We also had a simple Bible study to help us along the path of following Jesus, with a strong emphasis on listening to the Scripture and obeying its message.

OUR THREE FRUITS

As the leader/facilitator, I often reminded the group of our three purposes:

1. Learn to love Jesus more and grow closer to Jesus as disciples

2. Live as a spiritual family, caring for one another in the body of Christ

3. Be a blessing to our neighborhood in tangible ways

It wasn't always easy. As we got to know one another, we experienced some rocky times. We invited lots of people to come along, many of whom said no. In over a year, however, the group grew to about fifteen families. It was exactly what we envisioned: a dynamic family of spiritual brothers and sisters who loved one another and were committed to growing in their faith.

> **OUR GROUP BECAME A DYNAMIC FAMILY OF SPIRITUAL BROTHERS AND SISTERS WHO LOVED ONE ANOTHER AND WERE COMMITTED TO GROWING IN THEIR FAITH.**

Because of our desire for growth, we called the group the Community Garden.

Through this experience, I learned a great spiritual truth: It's always too soon to give up on God.

When George Müller was seeking God's direction in creating a new building to house orphans rather than continuing in rental homes, he had to wait on God in the fulfillment of the vision. It would be extremely costly. Confident that the vision was from the Lord, Müller asked God for provision.

Although no money was given for some time, Müller recalled:

> I was not discouraged by this, but trusted in the living God. We continued meeting for prayer morning by morning for fifteen days, but not a single donation came in; yet my heart was not discouraged. The more I prayed, the more assured I was that the Lord would give the means. Yea, as fully assured was I that the Lord would do so, as if I had already seen the new premises actually before me...my only motives were his honor and glory, and the welfare of the church of Christ at large, the real temporal and spiritual welfare of destitute orphans...finding that, after praying again and

again about the matter, I still remained in perfect peace, I judged it assuredly to be the will of God that I should go forward.[109]

The key to the kind of prayer Müller prayed was perseverance. If the vision were from God, Müller reasoned, God would make it happen.

A PRAYER FOR 63 YEARS

Müller prayed for sixty-three years for a friend's conversion. "The great point is never to give up until the answer comes," he said. "He is not converted yet, but he will be! How can it be otherwise? There is the unchanging promise of Jehovah, and on that I rest."

Just after Müller died—before his funeral—the friend finally came to the Lord.[110]

What is the desire of your heart? A second chance? A new career? The grace to forgive someone?

How many of your prayers go unanswered because you are unwilling to pray until God answers you?

HELPFUL PRAYER TOOLS

To persevere in prayer, one tool you can use is to write down your prayers. I've begun to keep a record of prayer requests. I sometimes go back and see what prayers have been answered. I have also been more aware of the frequency of praying for the same things over and over.

Some things on the list may not be answered for years and years. But I feel assurance that they will be answered—in God's way, in God's time.

Another tool to utilize is the gift of others' prayers. God honors the multiplication of prayers as believers commit to pray together and agree on the same things. Matthew 18:19 says, *"If two of you on earth agree about anything they ask for, it will be done for them by my Father in heaven."*

---

109. Müller, *The Life of Trust.*
110. George Müller, "God's Delays Are Not Denials," accessed August 25, 2021, www.georgemuller.org/quotes/category/gods-delays.

If your heart is broken for a son, daughter, or grandchild who has wandered far away from God, ask someone you trust to pray with you daily for that need. If you have a great dream in your heart that you know is from the Lord, ask others to join you in prayer.

I've found that when I ask others to pray with me about certain matters, circumstances start to break open that weren't possible before. I make it a point to check in periodically with these prayer partners to see if they have received a word of encouragement from the Lord or some insight that might lead to the prayer's fulfillment. Having more than one family committed to the mission of blessing people in our neighborhood was so encouraging to me. It wasn't the fullness of the prayer answered, but I saw that God was working. Others joined in praying for our neighbors. The garden grew.

How does your garden grow? Through persevering prayer.

Keep praying. Keep asking. Give thanks even when you don't feel like it. Believe God is working.

Above all, don't give up.

PRAYER PRINCIPLE #35:

It's always too soon to give up on God.

36

THE GIFT OF PRAYING LONG

I lay prostrate before the LORD those forty days and forty nights because the LORD had said he would destroy you. I prayed to the LORD and said, "Sovereign LORD, do not destroy your people, your own inheritance that you redeemed by your great power and brought out of Egypt with a mighty hand."
—Deuteronomy 9:25–26

I have run one full marathon in my life. Just one. My friend David said we should sign up together. "C'mon, it'll be fun," he said. Previously, I had only run a half marathon—thirteen miles.

But I agreed and started to train. Two weeks before the race, David backed out due to an injury. At that point, I had already trained for a twenty-mile run. I wanted to finish what I had started.

Three days before the race, the forecast called for light rain and cool temperatures. Three hours before the start time, it was freezing cold and raining cats and dogs with no sign of stopping.

I approached the starting line, already drenched and thinking about the four hours of running awaiting me. When the gun went off, I forced my legs to get moving. Taking longer than usual to warm up, I finally developed a good pace, but at mile 17, my legs started to cramp, and the pain continued through the rest of the race. At mile 22, I felt like I was going to throw up. But I kept going.

Even though David was injured, he brought his bike and met me at various spots along the course. "Keep going," he said. "You're looking good… That's great form. Keep moving."

When I approached the last half-mile, I saw my wife Jen and one of our kids, who came out to run the last stretch with me. I remember feeling completely drained and a little hypothermic. It was a grueling day. Although I was glad I had signed up and finished the race, I was *very* glad to cross the finish line.

SLOW TO START, QUICK TO FINISH

It's been said that people are slow to start and quick to finish when it comes to prayer. They struggle to connect with the Holy Spirit and eventually give up or must move on with their day. Even worse, people can develop patterns of prayer that last only a few minutes with very few results and only a measure of peace.

> *SOME OF OUR NEEDS AND DESIRES REQUIRE NOT QUICK, SPRINTING PRAYERS, BUT LONG, PERSEVERING, MARATHON PRAYERS.*

Some of our needs and desires, however, require not quick, sprinting prayers, but long, persevering, marathon prayers. Praying for a prodigal son or daughter to come home is like that. Praying for a better job while you endure a stressful work environment for your children's sake can be like that. Praying for a family member's salvation can be like that. Waiting for God to bless you with a child can be like that.

Romans 4:18 tells us that Abraham continued the journey of faith *"against all hope."* The promise of becoming the father of many nations was fulfilled even when the dream was seemingly all but dead.

MOSES PRAYS FOR HIS PEOPLE

Moses fasted and laid prostrate, praying for his people, for forty days and forty nights. (See Deuteronomy 9:18.) He felt led to pray at length because of the Hebrew people's audacious sin. While Moses was up on the mountain receiving the Ten Commandments, the Hebrews down in the valley lost their faith in the living God. They melted down their gold and fashioned a large idol, which looked like a golden calf. Then they bowed down to the idol and prayed for deliverance.

God was hot with anger, but then something miraculous happened. Moses said, *"The Lord listened to me"* (Deuteronomy 9:19). He reminded God, *"For they are your people and your heritage, whom you brought out* [of Egypt] *by your great power and by your outstretched arm"* (Deuteronomy 9:29 ESV).

God relented when Moses prayed. Amazing, right?

Do you believe that if you pray with faith and seek the Lord with all your heart, God not only hears but can also do something different than what He had planned? It may be that God intended all along to forgive the Hebrews. But surely God was pleased with Moses as he sought God's face on the people's behalf.

A PRAYER DURING POVERTY

In 1838, George Müller and his fellow workers were excessively impoverished. Although they saw God provide for them day by day, provision often came at the very last minute and only for bare necessities.

Müller reported:

The funds are exhausted. The laborers who had a little money have given as long as they had any left. Now observe how the Lord helped us! A lady from the neighborhood of London, who brought a parcel with money from her daughter, arrived four or five days since in Bristol, and took lodgings next door to the Boys' Orphan House. This afternoon she herself kindly brought me the money, amounting to three pounds two shillings and sixpence. We had been reduced so low as to be on the point of selling those things which could be spared; but this morning I had asked the Lord, if it might be, to prevent the necessity of our doing so. That the money had been so near the Orphan Houses for several days without being given, is a plain proof that it was from the beginning in the heart of God to help us; but, because he delights in the prayers of his children, he had allowed us to pray so long; also to try our faith, and to make the answer much the sweeter. It is indeed a precious deliverance. I burst out into loud praises and thanks the first moment I was alone after I had received the money.[111]

In essence, Müller was saying that having to pray for so long was a gift from God.

Sometimes God wants us to pray and pray to demonstrate our trust in Him. Long prayers reveal commitment. Long prayers embody faith even if what we seek is a long time coming or never comes all.

LONG PRAYERS EMBODY FAITH EVEN IF WHAT WE SEEK IS A LONG TIME COMING OR NEVER COMES ALL.

I hope that I can learn to pray longer over the course of my life. I hope that God will help me grow in trust and have the kind of faith that can pray for months, years, and even decades. I hope that each day I can spend more and more time in God's presence. I hope my faith will grow such that my biggest prayers will only increase my dependence on God and my belief that He is able to do what He says He will do.

What do you seek when you pray?

111. Müller, *The Life of Trust*.

246 PRAYER POWER

My one marathon was a miserable experience. Maybe one day, I will run another one. I do know that the training was worth it. Little by little, week by week, I became a stronger runner. I tested what I thought I could do and surpassed my expectations. The limitations weren't in my body, but in my brain.

So it is with the life of prayer.

People have told me, "Brent, I'm just not a person of prayer. I get easily distracted. I can't pray more than a few minutes." Others have said they just don't feel comfortable with prayer. They rarely entered into God's presence.

But prayer is the Christian's lifeline. There's no power without prayer. There's no discipleship without prayer. There's no real worship without prayer. There's no victory without prayer.

> **PRAYER IS THE CHRISTIAN'S LIFELINE. WITHOUT IT, THERE'S NO POWER, DISCIPLESHIP, REAL WORSHIP, OR VICTORY.**

If you don't believe that prayer is essential and ultimately for your good, then no amount of teaching will change your heart. Teaching only works where there's good soil and where life is able to grow. If you're a spiritual sluggard, none of this will make much sense.

But if you're open—if you say yes to the journey—if there is at least a little of Jesus's life flowing through your veins, then know that is God calling you to run an amazing race. God will give you the strength to run with endurance and one day cross the finish line. (See Hebrews 12:1–2.)

THREE WAYS TO RUN YOUR RACE

Here are a few ways you can start training for that adventure.

1. Start to incrementally increase your morning or evening routine in prayer. Some of the world's greatest athletes follow the *1 percent*

principle. They try to get a little better by just 1 percent each day. Add a few minutes to your daily prayers. Like compound interest, your prayer life can grow in just a month's time.

2. Set a day aside for extended prayer. Take a day in the woods. Go alone if you feel safe, or take a friend, but ask for silence throughout the day. See if you could pray for a full hour, for two hours, or even six or eight hours.

3. Commit to an extended period of prayer like Moses did. Fast from something for forty days and seek to deepen your prayer life during that time.

Don't choose all three of those. Pick one. Pursue it with passion.

Soon you'll be reaching milestones you thought were insurmountable. Soon you'll be praying with more power.

You will have learned how to pray long.

PRAYER PRINCIPLE #36:

Long prayers lead to big victories.

37

RESCUE HERO

Pray in the Spirit on all occasions with all kinds of prayers and requests. With this in mind, be alert and always keep on praying for all the Lord's people.
—Ephesians 6:18

You probably have never heard of Dave Karnes. During the terrorist attacks on September 11, 2001, when everyone else was running away from danger in New York City, he ran toward the danger. Only twenty survivors were pulled from the rubble of the World Trade Center after the towers fell. Two of the last three were not saved by a firefighter, rescue worker, or police officer. They were rescued by Dave Karnes.[112]

When the first plane hit, Karnes was in Wilton, Connecticut, where he worked as a senior accountant. When the second plane hit, Karnes told his colleagues, "We're at war." He had spent twenty-three years in the Marine Corps and felt it was his duty to help. He told his boss he might be gone for a while.

---

112. Rebecca Liss, "An Unlikely Hero," *Slate*, September 11, 2015, accessed August 25, 2021, slate.com/news-and-politics/2015/09/the-marine-who-found-two-wtc-survivors.html.

PREPARING FOR A RESCUE MISSION

Then he went to get a haircut. "Give me a good Marine Corps squared-off haircut," he told the barber. And even though he was no longer an active Marine, he went home to put on his military fatigues and then collected rappelling gear, ropes, and other equipment from a storage unit. He was preparing for a rescue mission.

The next stop was his church. A devout Christian, Karnes asked the pastor and parishioners who had gathered after the attack to say a prayer that God would give him strength and guidance to find survivors.

He sped toward New York, praying that his fatigues, haircut, and equipment would be enough to get him to the crash site. It worked. Around 5:30 p.m., he was waved past the barricades. Emergency personnel had just been ordered away because the site was unstable. Flames and smoke made many areas unapproachable.

Undeterred, Karnes and another Marine climbed over the tangled steel and began looking into openings. Over and over, they yelled, "United States Marines. If you can hear us, yell or tap!"

After about an hour of searching, Karnes heard a muffled voice. Will Jimeno and John McLoughlin, two Port Authority officers, were buried twenty feet below the surface. For nearly ten hours, they had been waiting for help, thirsty and in terrible pain, amid debris, dust, and smoke.

Like Karnes, Jimeno was a man of faith. He had been praying for rescue. When he was just about ready to give up, he had a vision of Jesus.[113]

Jimeno and McLoughlin were finally freed from the rubble after several hours of digging.

Two men of faith were trusting in God—one was a rescuer, the other sought rescue. One was used by God to walk by faith past the flames and the smoke; the other was empowered to cling to faith under the rubble. Both men depended on prayer through the Holy Spirit.

When you feel overwhelmed, where do you turn?

---

113. "Will Jimeno Prepares to Die on 9/11 at the World Trade Center," www.mossyoak.com/our-obsession/blogs/prostaff/will-jimeno-prepares-to-die-on-9-11-at-the-world-trade-center.

Whether you're facing the day-to-day challenges of life or are over-whelmed by life's circumstances, you need strength to keep going. You cannot strengthen yourself in these moments of crisis. The human tendency is to overwork or overthink, to try to manage or strategize our way out of trouble. However, the way to access God's power is not through more strategy or human effort, but through more surrender.

> **THE WAY TO ACCESS GOD'S POWER IS NOT THROUGH MORE STRATEGY OR HUMAN EFFORT, BUT THROUGH MORE SURRENDER.**

In spiritual terms, surrender is complete dependence on God. It's a posture that constantly turns to God for help. Paul says, *"Be strong in the Lord and in his mighty power"* (Ephesians 6:10). That's the real source of strength.

PUT ON THE ARMOR OF GOD

How do we access that power? Paul counsels people of faith to put on the full armor of God: the belt of truth, breastplate of righteousness, shoes of readiness to proclaim the gospel, the shield of faith, the helmet of salvation, and the sword of the Spirit. (See Ephesians 6:14–17.) Then Paul says, *"Pray in the Spirit on all occasions with all kinds of prayers and requests"* (Ephesians 6:18).

> **GOD'S STRENGTH IS ACCESSED WHEN WE SEEK TO EQUIP OURSELVES WITH FAITH IN CHRIST AND PRAY IN THE SPIRIT'S POWER NO MATTER WHAT IS HAPPENING.**

In other words, God's strength is accessed when we seek daily to equip ourselves with faith in Christ and pray in the Spirit's power no matter what is happening. Our conversations with the Lord should include *"all kinds of prayers"* that represent the fullness of our relationship with God. That means that our prayers should include praise, petition, intercession, confession, and thanksgiving.

That's how George Müller prayed. He knew what it was to feel weak and powerless. He knew what it felt like to be buried under the rubble of poverty and responsibility. Therefore, he repeatedly went to the Source, not only in the morning but also throughout the day and night. Whether he was launching a building campaign for a new orphanage or simply asking for daily bread for the children under his care, he knew that he needed God's help.

Müller wrote:

> Straits and difficulties I expected from the very beginning. Before I began this service I expected them; nay, the chief object of it was, that the church at large might be strengthened in faith, and be led more simply, habitually, and unreservedly to trust in the living God, by seeing his hand stretched out in my behalf in the hour of need.[114]

This kind of prayer is both hard and easy. On the one hand, it takes intentionality and discipline to pray about all things with all types of prayers. It means forsaking dependence on other forms of strength to seize the greatest source of strength, which is God. On the other hand, this kind of prayer is easy in that it simplifies one's life approach. There is only one real place to go for help.

The greater the trials, the greater the need for trust.

Where do you need God's hand to reach down into your life?

A DAILY SELF-CHECK

Maybe it's in your habits. Your poor discipline may be draining you spiritually. Your activities may be making you spiritually dull. I heard about a pastor who uses the acronym "RMPS" every day to a conduct of self-check.

---

114. Müller, *The Life of Trust.*

- *R* stands for relationships. This pastor asks himself, "How am I doing with my key relationships? Am I paying enough attention to the people I love the most or those I feel called to serve?"

- *M* stands for mental. "Am I staying mentally strong? Am I putting good things in my mind? Am I reading in a way that helps me grow?"

- *P* stands for physical. "Am I taking care of my body, exercising and staying fit to serve the Lord?"

- *S* stands for spiritual. "Am I praying and trusting God more each day? Am I studying God's Word to learn about the heart of God?"

These habits lead to good results. They prepare the pastor for whatever challenge might come his way. I can't help but think that as he disciplines himself, God gives him more tasks to fulfill.

Maybe you need God's hand to reach down when it comes to forgiveness. You may have been holding a grudge for too long. You may need a heart change. You may need to be reminded that God forgives you of every sin. If so, you must forgive others of their sins.

Maybe you need God's hand to reach down and help you through difficult circumstances. You may feel buried under the rubble of too many challenges. You may wonder where you'll get the strength to press on.

Isaiah 40:31 holds a wonderful promise: *"Those who hope in the Lord will renew their strength. They will soar on wings like eagles; they will run and not grow weary, they will walk and not be faint."*

Both Karnes and Jimeno learned that God *"gives strength to the weary and increases the power of the weak"* (Isaiah 40:29).

PRAY IN ALL THINGS

Today, start a practice of praying in all things, in as many ways as you can pray. Give yourself reminders to pray. Reach out to friends and ask for prayer.

Before long, you'll connect with the living God who is also called *Yahweh*, meaning "God saves" or "God rescues." God's strength will flow into your life as His hand reaches into your worst circumstances or spiritual challenges.

Prayer starts with surrender.

An old hymn tells us, "Satan trembles when he sees the weakest Christian on their knees."

Get into your private place of prayer. Drop to your knees. Lift your hands to the living God. See what God can do.

PRAYER PRINCIPLE #37:

When you reach up, God reaches down.

38

THE CLIMB

Jesus went out to a mountainside to pray, and spent the night
praying to God.
—Luke 6:12

George Mallory may have been the first mountain climber to reach the top of Mount Everest. In the early 1920s, he led a number of attempts to scale the mountain, eventually being killed during the third attempt in 1924. His body was found in 1999, well preserved by the snow and ice.

They found him 2,700 feet up the mountain, just 2,000 feet from the peak. The posture of his body suggested that he never gave up. He was face down on a rocky slope, head toward the summit. His arms were extended high over his head. His toes were pointed into the mountain. His fingers dug into the loose rock, as if he refused to let go, even as he drew his last breath.[115]

---

115. Katie Serena, "See the Moment Hikers Discovered George Mallory's Body on Mount Everest [Video]," *ATI*, November 16, 2017, accessed August 25, 2021, allthatsinteresting.com/george-mallory-body.

THE JOY OF THE CLIMB

In 1922, when Mallory was asked why he was attempting to climb Mount Everest, he replied:

There is not the slightest prospect of any gain whatsoever. Oh, we may learn a little about the behavior of the human body at high altitudes, and possibly medical men may turn our observation to some account for the purposes of aviation. But otherwise nothing will come of it. We shall not bring back a single bit of gold or silver, not a gem, nor any coal or iron. We shall not find a single foot of earth that can be planted with crops to raise food. It's no use. So, if you cannot understand that there is something in man which responds to the challenge of this mountain and goes out to meet it, that the struggle is the struggle of life itself upward and forever upward, then you won't see why we go. What we get from this adventure is just sheer joy. And joy is, after all, the end of life. We do not live to eat and make money. We eat and make money to be able to enjoy life. That is what life means and what life is for.[116]

On many occasions, Jesus climbed a mountain to pray. The gospels tell us that He went up the mountain when faced with a big decision, or when He was under a great deal of stress, or simply when He needed to hear His Father's voice. He brought every need, thought, and concern to God.

> ON MANY OCCASIONS, JESUS CLIMBED A MOUNTAIN TO PRAY. HE BROUGHT EVERY NEED, THOUGHT, AND CONCERN TO HIS FATHER.

116. George Mallory, quoted in "Climbing Mount Everest is Work for Supermen," *The New York Times*, March 18, 1923, accessed August 25, 2021, www.nytimes.com/1923/03/18/archives/climbing-mount-everest-is-work-for-supermen-a-member-of-former.html.

Sometimes I have wondered, *Why did Jesus pray? Wasn't He fully God and fully human? Wasn't He always connected to His heavenly Father?*

Perhaps the answer is found in why we pray. What purposes do we have in prayer? Did Jesus pray for the same reasons?

We could certainly say that we may pray like children bringing their needs before their heavenly Father. We could also say that prayer is the way we recalibrate our lives toward God's will. Even more, we could say that we draw near to God so that we will be transformed into the likeness of Jesus.

PRAYER IS A GIFT

But more and more, I believe that prayer is a gift, like a mighty mountain before us. God invites us to come toward, near, and finally into God's presence. We're invited into the great mystery of communing with the divine. If we embark on the journey of scaling the mountain of prayer, we can believe that we will find what we seek.

In that way, prayer is the struggle of life itself, forever upward. The pinnacle is joy. The purpose is peace. I believe that is also why Jesus prayed. He found joy and peace when He prayed.

George Müller also spent time in daily prayer, rising early and then pausing throughout the day to pray for specific needs. He faced many challenges throughout his ministry, from poverty to business troubles to threats on his life. Müller found that prayer and faith could overcome any obstacle.

MÜLLER'S STRUGGLES IN PRAYER

For the first ten years of what he called his "life of faith," however, Müller struggled in prayer. He often didn't feel like praying. He had a hard time getting into the spirit of prayer. Then just a slight shift in the way he prayed made all the difference. This is how he described it:

The difference, then, between my former practice and my present one is this: Formerly, when I rose, I began to pray as soon as possible, and generally spent all my time till breakfast in prayer, or almost all the time. At all events I almost invariably began with prayer, except when I felt my soul to be more than usually barren, in which case I read the word of God for food, or for refreshment, or for a revival and renewal of my inner man, before I gave myself to prayer. But what was the result? I often spent a quarter of an hour, or half an hour, or even an hour, on my knees, before being conscious to myself of having derived comfort, encouragement, humbling of soul…and often, after having suffered much from wandering of mind for the first ten minutes, or a quarter of an hour, or even half an hour, I only then began really to pray. I scarcely ever suffer now in this way. For my heart being nourished by the truth, being brought into experimental fellowship with God, I speak to my Father and to my Friend (vile though I am, and unworthy of it) about the things that he has brought before me in his precious word. It often now astonishes me that I did not sooner see this point.[117]

Sometimes Müller's mind or heart would wander and even though he truly wanted to pray, he struggled to focus his thoughts and spark feelings for prayer in his heart. Only after a spiritual battle would he be able to enter into a divine connection with the living God. The pairing of Scripture and prayer helped him attain God's presence. But it wasn't easy.

You may ask, "Why does prayer have to be a struggle? Why doesn't God make it easier to connect with Him, given that He constantly tells us in Scripture to come to Him, to cast our burdens on Him, and depend on Him?"

THE PROBLEM IS NOT GOD BUT OUR FALLEN WORLD. OUR LIVES ARE FULL OF DISTRACTIONS, WORRIES, AND HEARTACHES, TAKING US AWAY FROM THE LIVING GOD.

The problem is not God but our fallen world. Our lives are full of distractions, worries, and heartaches, taking us away from the living God.

---

117. Müller, *The Life of Trust*.

Our whole lives are a struggle upward. We may think that prayer should not be a relentless expedition, but that's often the way it feels.

On the other side of the struggle, something beautiful emerges. Müller learned that the more time one spends in prayer and the more one exercises faith in prayer, the more meaningful and even breathtaking the experience becomes.

HEARING FROM GOD

One summer, I decided I needed to climb a mountain. I had been pondering a big decision for several months. When I started the journey upward, I had no idea regarding God's direction for my life. I needed peace. I needed to hear from God.

Starting out at the Alum Cave Trailhead in the Great Smoky Mountains National Park, I steadily climbed five miles to the peak of Mount Leconte. Rain fell hard and created rivulets along the path all the way up. Fog prevented the magnificent views I had anticipated. However, when I got to the peak, in deep cloud cover with the wind howling around me, I met my heavenly Father. He spoke to me about living with passion, not being afraid, and trusting Him for whatever the journey ahead would be.

I see myself as someone who is learning to pray. I have a long way to go. I have experienced something akin to George Mallory's pursuit of the peak of Mount Everest. I'm learning George Müller's pursuit of power in prayer. I'm discovering that prayer is not so much about having my needs met as it is about seeking God's face. It's about hearing from God, touching God, seeing God, and experiencing God.

PRAYER IS NOT SO MUCH ABOUT HAVING OUR NEEDS MET AS IT IS ABOUT SEEKING GOD'S FACE, HEARING FROM HIM, AND EXPERIENCING HIM.

You may find yourself in a struggle when you seek God in this way, but God will help you in the climb toward His presence.

Ole Hallesby, a Norwegian pastor of the early 20th century, said, "My helpless friend, your helplessness is the most powerful plea which rises up to the tender father-heart of God. He has heard your prayer from the very first moment that you honestly cried to Him in your need, and night and day He inclines His ear toward earth in order to ascertain if there are any helpless mortals turning to Him in their distress...You think that everything is closed to you because you cannot pray. My friend, your helplessness is the very essence of prayer."[118]

I met God on the mountain, just as Jesus did. Maybe you need to meet God on your mountain, whether it's physical or metaphorical.

Begin the climb today.

Joy awaits.

PRAYER PRINCIPLE #38:

God's presence is worth every struggle we encounter in prayer.

118. Ole Hallesby, *Prayer* (Minneapolis, MN: Augsburg Fortress Publishing, 1994), 22.

39

THE DOOR RIGHT
IN FRONT OF YOU

*Rejoice in the Lord always. I will say it again: Rejoice! Let your
gentleness be evident to all. The Lord is near. Do not be anxious
about anything, but in every situation, by prayer and petition, with
thanksgiving, present your requests to God.*
—Philippians 4:4–6

Several years ago, I helped a church start an evening prayer gathering.
I had big dreams and high hopes. I imagined hundreds of people praising, bringing their every need before the Lord, and lifting others in prayer.
After all, believers should want to pray, right? Don't we profess the power
of prayer? Don't we yearn to be in the presence of God?

We set the time, developed a format, had a lot of publicity, and
launched the service. Sadly, very few people showed up. I was perplexed
and a little discouraged. Several hundred people gathered for worship on
Sunday. Why was it hard to gather for prayer on Tuesday evenings? As
the weeks passed, there were rarely more than a few dozen present. Some
weeks, only a handful came.

A SMALL BUT POWERFUL GROUP

For those who participated, however, it was an amazing experience. Over several years, God knit that small group together in powerful ways. There is nothing like real, extended prayer with other believers. Once someone got in the habit of attending the prayer service, they rarely missed a night. Praying together became not just an optional activity, but a life-giving part of the flow of the week. Although my expectations were not met, I never regretted initiating those services. The effort was worthwhile because I always left those services feeling encouraged and refreshed by the Holy Spirit.

> **ON SOME NIGHTS, IT FELT AS IF HEAVEN'S GATES OPENED AS WE PRAYED FOR HEALING, HUMBLENESS IN WORSHIP, AND REVIVAL FOR OUR COUNTRY.**

In the first weeks we started to meet, we asked the Lord, *"Teach us to pray"* (Luke 11:1). We knew we needed to learn how to pray just as the first disciples did. On some nights, it felt as if heaven's gates opened as we prayed for healing, humbleness in worship, and revival for our country. God taught me and others so much about prayer in those times together.

Still, I wondered, *Why don't more people want to pray?*

I know people pray in private. I know they pray in Sunday school classes and small groups. I know people believe in prayer. So, why can't people carve out just one hour to pray with other believers?

I believe it mostly has to do with how people understand prayer. Many people see prayer as important, but perhaps not as valuable as, say, serving other people or spending time with family. Some people don't know how to pray and can't imagine sitting for an hour, feeling uncomfortable and wondering, *What should I be feeling now?*

FINDING JOY IN PRAYER

There's one more reason, however, that people don't pray. Some see prayer as always serious and grim. There's no *joy*. Two words that don't often go together are *joy* and *prayer*. Many people think of prayer as really serious business. And if asked to come to a prayer meeting on Tuesday evenings, they would imagine a cheerless, solemn fellowship that involved moving through a prayer list of people's aches and pains. They would think it would be boring, dull, or ritualized. It's no wonder people don't want to pray.

> **MANY PEOPLE THINK OF PRAYER AS REALLY SERIOUS BUSINESS AND ENVISION A PRAYER MEETING AS BORING, DULL, OR RITUALIZED.**

When Jesus drove the money changers from the temple, He quoted a portion of Isaiah 56:7: *"My house will be called a house of prayer for all nations."* However, the whole verse says so much more.

Envisioning foreigners coming from all over the world to the place of prayer, God says through the prophet Isaiah, *"These I will bring to my holy mountain and give them joy in my house of prayer. Their burnt offerings and sacrifices will be accepted on my altar; for my house will be called a house of prayer for all nations."*

Jesus quoted the passage from Isaiah because He was angry with what the temple had become, but His ultimate motive was that people from all over the world would experience the joy of prayer.

REJOICE ALWAYS

Because joy and prayer belong together, Paul wrote, *"Rejoice always, pray continually, give thanks in all circumstances; for this is God's will for you in Christ Jesus"* (1 Thessalonians 5:16–18). In reading these verses, many people wonder how it's possible to pray continuously; however, they miss the first verse that says to rejoice or be joyful *always*.

People hear the call to prayer, but not the call to joy.

George Müller loved to pray. He brought everything—material needs, spiritual concerns, and relationship issues—before the Lord in prayer. He was willing to wait in prayer for long periods of time. He looked for answers and expected help. When God sent help, Müller gave thanks and experienced the joy of heaven.

He wrote, "The joy that answers to prayer give cannot be described, and the impetus that they afford to the spiritual life is exceedingly great. I desire the experience of this happiness for all my Christian readers."[119]

Life is hard. Sometimes our prayers are full of anxiety and even tears. I wonder if we miss the central truth—that we have been given the gift of prayer so that we can experience great joy in our heavenly Father's presence.

> **WE HAVE BEEN GIVEN THE GIFT OF PRAYER SO THAT WE CAN EXPERIENCE GREAT JOY IN OUR HEAVENLY FATHER'S PRESENCE.**

When I was growing up, I never saw anyone pray with great joy. I never heard anyone talk about prayer as anything other than serious. Prayer was a duty to fulfill. As an adult, however, I met some people who knew how to pray with joy. They had chosen to be joyful first rather than waiting for God to fix their circumstances. The joy of the Lord is their strength. (See Nehemiah 8:10.) That joy made them want to come again and again into God's presence.

How about you? Is that your experience in prayer? Do you want it to be?

HOW TO PRAY WITH JOY

Let me offer a few ideas to help you pray with joy.

Start with gratitude and rejoicing in the Lord. Thank God for what He is doing in your life. Giving thanks, focusing on the positive ways that God is working.

119. Müller, *Release the Power of Prayer*, 74.

Next, be real before your heavenly Father. Ask for what you need. Make yourself vulnerable. Be honest. Say what's on your heart. God doesn't want to hear about what you think ought to be in you. God wants to hear what is really in you.

I grew up with a kind of moral performance Christianity. I showed up and put on a smile. I was taught not to talk about the doubts I might have or how I had failed. I learned to approach God not out of need, but with a desire to impress Him. As an adult, I knew that I needed to learn to pray differently, to recognize my total dependence on God.

Just be yourself. God knows the real you anyway. You don't have to recount the story of Moses and the prophets, with *thees* and *thous*. Speak from your heart. When you say the same prayer over and over, with the same tone and the same words, it's probably not coming from the heart.

Finally, keep it simple. Some people pray like they're working through their grocery list of names and needs. There's nothing wrong with that approach. However, Jesus said that your heavenly Father knows what you need. Therefore, you don't have to say a lot of words. Stick to the basics. Focus on communing with God.

YOUR HEAVENLY FATHER KNOWS WHAT YOU NEED. YOU DON'T HAVE TO SAY A LOT OF WORDS. FOCUS ON COMMUNING WITH GOD.

The more I learn about prayer, the less I say. The more I listen, the longer I want to spend in God's presence.

Taking hold of joy reminds me of times when my dad would let me take the steering wheel of the car when I was a kid. I would sit next to him as he was driving down the interstate. He would ask, "Do you want to drive?" Before I could answer, he would take his hands off the wheel. I grabbed the wheel as Dad kept his foot on the gas, sometimes accelerating just for fun. It was thrilling to steer the car. But when we would come to a turn or approach another car, he would take the wheel again while my hands were still on it. If I got too scared, all I had to say was, "Daddy, take the wheel!"

There are times when I feel so burdened that all I can say is, "Lord, I need You here. I need You to take the wheel. I don't know what is going to happen; but I trust You, and I believe that You can fill me with joy even in the worst of circumstances."

God waits for you to turn to Him.

WHEN ONE DOOR SHUTS...

One day I was working in my home office in Dallas. We lived in a hundred-year-old house, with the original doors and door handles. When my wife Jen came in to tell me goodbye on her way to the store, she shut my office door behind her. The doorknob popped off on my side. I didn't think much about it—that happened frequently—but when I got up to get some coffee, I realized I was locked in my office. I tried to work the lock without the doorknob, but I knew it would only open from the other side.

Annoyed, I texted Jen, saying, "When are you going to come home? I'm locked in my office." I waited a minute for her response. She then texted back, "Have you tried the other door to your office?" The second door opened to the back porch. Embarrassed, I opened that door, stepped onto the porch, and made my way around the house to come back inside.

Sometimes I do the dumbest things and wonder, *When will I get it right?* Sometimes I get so upset by all of life's circumstances and frustrations that I can't even see what's in front of me. I search for a solution, but the way out is there all along.

Prayer is the door that God wants us to enter again and again—vulnerably, simply, and joyfully.

Choose joy. Rejoice always. Pray with joy.

PRAYER PRINCIPLE #39:

True prayer always leads to true joy.

40

YOUR ONE WILD
AND PRECIOUS LIFE

Because he bends down to listen,
I will pray as long as I have breath!
—Psalm 116:2 (NLT)

If Jesus had taken fifteen breaths per minute over his earthly life of thirty-three years, He would have taken 260,172,000 breaths. His first breath was in a stable in Bethlehem and His final breath was on a cross in Jerusalem.

Sometimes I think about all that Jesus did with His breaths. He prayed to His heavenly Father, taught people about God, healed the sick, and even raised more than one person from the dead. He gathered a new spiritual family and launched a worldwide movement of disciples who would follow His way.

If God allows me to have seventy-two years on earth, I will have breathed 567,648,000 breaths. My first breath was taken in Birmingham, Alabama. Only God knows where I will take my last breath, but if I have any say in the matter, it will be in Tennessee.

Our lives have a beginning and an end. When we are born, we take our first breath. When we die, we will take our last breath. The question is, *What will we do with the breath we have been given?*

A DASH BETWEEN TWO DATES

The poem "How to Live With Your Dash" is about a man who spoke at the funeral of a good friend. He talked about the day of her birth and the day that she died. Those two dates would be etched on her tombstone. In between would be a dash. The friend said that it was not the beginning or the end that made the woman who she was. It was the dash.

Your life is made of two dates and a dash. The dash between the two dates means so much. The dash is full of first days of school, graduations, maybe getting married, fun times with family and friends, dressing up for Halloween, Thanksgivings and Christmases and Easters, family vacations, weddings, births, deaths, good times, and bad times. The dash includes times you wish you could go back and relive. It also includes times you wish you could forget. That dash is such a small thing on a tombstone but is by far the most important part. The poem concludes:

So, when your eulogy is being read

With your life's actions to rehash…

Would you be proud of the things they say

About how you spent YOUR dash?[120]

How will you live your dash? Will you invest in relationships? Will you learn how to follow Christ to experience His abundant life? Will you learn to pray? Will you find the joy that comes from serving others and serving Jesus? Or will you serve yourself? How will you spend the precious breath that God has given to you?

HOW WILL YOU LIVE YOUR DASH? HOW WILL YOU SPEND THE PRECIOUS BREATH THAT GOD HAS GIVEN TO YOU?

120. Linda Ellis, "The Dash," lifeism.co/the-dash-poem-by-linda-ellis.

After launching orphanages that served more than 10,000 children, raising his daughter Lydia, traveling the world to preach, supporting missionaries, and supplying Scriptures and tracts for more than 50,000 people, George Müller came to the end of his life.

A BRIGHT PROSPECT AWAITS

It was Holy Week. On Sunday, March 6, 1898, Müller spoke at Alma Road Chapel. His text was from John 12, which describes Jesus's anointing and triumphal entry into Jerusalem. Müller spoke of the "bright prospect" of heaven that Christians can anticipate. The following Wednesday, he told James Wright, his son-in-law and successor in running the orphanages, that he was feeling weak and needed rest. In the evening, however, he held his usual prayer meeting at the Orphan House. They concluded with the hymn, "We'll Sing of the Shepherd That Died."

The next morning, March 10, 1898, Müller awoke between five and six o'clock. He got up and walked to the dressing table. It was then that the "bright prospect" he had spoken about in his sermon just four days earlier became a glorious reality. Müller met the Savior he had served for seventy years.[121]

Years before he took his final breath, Müller said, "The longer I live, the more I am enabled to realize that I have but one life to live on earth, and that this one life is but a brief life, for sowing, in comparison with eternity, for reaping."[122]

He lived his life to the full for Christ. His dash made an eternal difference. Most of all, he learned to pray and depend on his heavenly Father. He led others to know that they, too, could pray to God and see Him work in miraculous ways.

Müller often remarked that his life was not extraordinary. Others could experience the same quiet trust, joyful faith, and expectant answers to prayer. He observed, "Every child of God is not called by the Lord to establish schools and orphan houses, and to trust in the Lord for means

---

121. Roger Steer, "Delighted in God," *Christian History Institute*, 2018, accessed August 25, 2021, christianhistoryinstitute.org/magazine/article/delighted-in-god.
122. Arthur Pierson, *George Müller of Bristol* (Grand Rapids, MI: Kregel Classics, 1999), 431.

for them; yet there is nothing on the part of the Lord to hinder, why you may not know, by experience, far more abundantly than we do now, his willingness to answer the prayers of his children."[123]

What about your life? No matter how you have lived up until now, how do you want to use the breath that you have left?

To experience Jesus's full life and to be used for His glory, there must be a kind of death before the day you die. You must die to yourself so that His life can be lived through you.

Müller once said, "There was a day when I died, utterly died to George Müller, his opinions, preferences, tastes, and will—died to the world, its approval or censure—died to the approval or blame of even my brethren and friends—and since then I have studied to show myself approved unto God."[124]

Jesus said, *"Whoever wants to be my disciple must deny themselves and take up their cross daily and follow me"* (Luke 9:23). Dying to yourself means that you let go of your wants, your preferences, and your ego so that God can reign in your heart. It doesn't mean you stop enjoying life. Instead, God gives you a new life that reorients you to serving God and others—leading to lasting peace and happiness.

JESUS CALLS US TO TAKE UP OUR CROSSES DAILY. EVERY DAY, WE NEED TO EXPERIENCE A KIND OF MINI-DEATH SO THAT GOD'S WAY CAN BE PURSUED.

On several occasions, I knew that I needed to die to myself on a new level. I thought I had surrendered to God, but then I discovered some area of my life not completely devoted to Him. This, I believe, is why Jesus calls us to take up our crosses daily. Every day, we need to experience a kind of

---

123. Müller, *The Life of Trust.*
124. Roger Steer, "George Müller, Did You Know?" *Christian History Institute,* accessed August 25, 2021, christianhistoryinstitute.org/magazine/article/did-you-know-mueller.

mini-death so that God's way can be pursued. There are also watershed moments when you commit your life to Christ on a new level.

One of my mentors said that he experienced such a moment when he was a young man. God had called him to pastor a church, but he sensed that God was calling him to a smaller church, for less income. He faced a decision. Would he die to himself, or would he pursue the path that led to more worldly success? He remembered something his own mentor shared: "There comes a moment when you must put the full weight of your life on Jesus Christ or live forever as a coward." He chose to trust Jesus and went to the smaller church. It was the beginning of a new and very fruitful season of ministry. He learned to love people. He learned to pray with greater trust.

When you die to yourself, God can begin to teach you to really pray. Your every breath becomes an opportunity to draw near to the living God.

MADE FOR GOD'S GLORY

Use your life for a big purpose. You were made for God's glory. Your own glory is too small a thing to live for. God continues to give you breath for a reason. It's not too late to be close to God. It's not too late to learn to pray. It's not too late to start serving others.

My favorite poet, Mary Oliver, wrote a beautiful poem called "The Summer Day." It reads in part:

> I don't know exactly what a prayer is.
>
> I do know how to pay attention, how to fall down
>
> into the grass, how to kneel down in the grass,
>
> how to be idle and blessed, how to stroll through the fields,
>
> which is what I have been doing all day.
>
> Tell me, what else should I have done?
>
> Doesn't everything die at last, and too soon?
>
> Tell me, what is it you plan to do

with your one wild and precious life?[125]

Sometimes I feel like Mary Oliver does. Sometimes I really don't know what a prayer is or what happens when I pray. But I have come to see that it's more about paying attention and beholding the living God than it is asking for things and waiting for answers. It's about lingering in God's presence. Prayer is about life—real life. This life is precious. For those who let go and trust, life can be a wild, beautiful adventure.

One day, your life will be over. One day, you will also breathe your last breath. Don't waste what you have been given.

God is bending down to hear you today. Get alone with God and pray that He will give you clarity on your life. Let your heavenly Father surround you with love. Ask God to help you to dedicate your life from this day forward, to serve Him, and to live for His glory.

PRAYER PRINCIPLE #40:

Every breath is another opportunity to pray.

---

125. Mary Oliver, "A Summer Day," from *New and Selected Poems* (Boston, MA: Beacon Press, 1992).

ABOUT THE AUTHOR

Dr. Brent Patrick McDougal is the senior pastor of the First Baptist Church of Knoxville, Tennessee. Each Sunday, he speaks to about 3,000 people through in-person, television, and online worship.

Brent received his B.A. in Religion/Political Science from Emory University and a Master of Divinity from Beeson Divinity School of Samford University. He also holds a Ph.D. in Political Science from the University of Alabama, a cross-discipline study of politics and religion.

Brent is the author of *The River of the Soul* and *Faith, Hope and Politics*. He has written numerous guest blog posts and articles, including "America's Spiritual Pandemic" for *Christianity Today*.

A native of Alabama, Brent has a heart for bringing people together, cultivating atmospheres of prayer. and encouraging devotion among church members as well as throughout the community at large. Prior to joining the First Baptist Church of Knoxville, he served in Alabama and Texas.

In various ministry settings, Brent has been involved with launching significant prayer movements. Most recently, he started DallasPrays, an ecumenical call to city-wide prayer that included devotional writing, weekly prayer calls, and events that brought people together to pray for city transformation.

Brent and his wife Jennifer have two grown children, Christopher and Emily.